The Politics of Volunteering

Political Sociology Series

Daniel Béland, *What is Social Policy?
Understanding the Welfare State*

Nina Eliasoph, *The Politics of Volunteering*

Hank Johnston, *States & Social Movements*

Richard Lachmann, *States and Power*

The Politics of Volunteering

Nina Eliasoph

polity

First published in 2013 by Polity Press

Polity Press
65 Bridge Street
Cambridge CB2 1UR, UK

Polity Press
350 Main Street
Malden, MA 02148, USA

ISBN-13: 978-0-7456-5003-6 (hardback)
ISBN-13: 978-0-7456-5004-3(paperback)

A catalogue record for this book is available from the British Library.

Typeset in 11 on 13 pt Sabon
by Servis Filmsetting Ltd, Stockport, Cheshire
Printed and bound by the MPG Printgroup, UK

For further information on Polity, visit our website: www.politybooks.com

Contents

v

Introduction:
What Are Civic Associations?

You have probably done some volunteer work. Maybe you did it because you cared about someone. Maybe it was a requirement for high-school graduation. Maybe you needed a line on your CV, to demonstrate to future employers that you were a good person, or maybe you needed some good, unpaid work experience. Maybe you were amazed at how much you helped someone, or how much you learned. Maybe you secretly wondered if you were doing any good for anyone at all.

Less likely is the possibility that you engaged in political activism, trying to change society in a more dramatic way than a volunteer usually does. Usually, volunteering offers the possibility for people to give hands-on, immediate help for the needy – food, blankets, help learning to read. Activists usually aim to change broader social conditions, so that people are not so needy in the first place, but already have enough food, enough blankets, and enough help learning to read. Sometimes, activists criticize volunteers for putting band-aids on problems that require surgery.

Probably, you have never heard anyone say anything critical about volunteers, but lately, a few people have started to murmur some doubts about the proliferation of volunteer projects around the world. When, for example, a corporate polluter stages a splashy volunteer event, critics say it is designed to whitewash the oil spills away. When you are forced to volunteer, critics call it an oxymoron. When well-meaning volunteers devote themselves to feeding the homeless, while voting for policies that cut aid for housing, critics point out the discrepancy.

In these and other ways, volunteering is starting to become controversial. Are any of the critics' doubts valid? What trends are shaping volunteer work today? Why would activists ever scorn volunteers? Is there a way to strike a balance between the goods that come from volunteering and the goods that come from political activism? To answer these questions, we first have to understand why most of us put so much stock in volunteering and in the importance of non-governmental organizations. The volunteer is a figure that is, in our imaginations, so pure, it is almost impossible to imagine a harmful one. Yet, sometimes, volunteers can do great harm. This book opens up the question of how volunteers and NGOs can do harm, as well as tremendous good. What makes civic life effective? What can kill effective civic life? What brings it to life?

Chapter 1 examines the theories and beliefs that lead so many people to treat the volunteer as a near-sacred figure. A thread running through our answers to this question is a comparison between two common forms of *civic association*: volunteering and political activism. While volunteers often try to separate their work from "politics," and just to concentrate on helping individuals one at a time, chapter 1 will also show how volunteering can sometimes lead people to pose bigger questions about how our society works. Sometimes, that is, volunteers start off serving meals to the hungry and then go further, to ask why a wealthy society like ours even has hungry people to begin with. In other words, the volunteer starts to realize that helping individuals requires not just one-on-one volunteer work, but political activism, as well.

Using examples from the disability rights movement, the anti-domestic violence movement, Occupy Wall Street, and other civic associations, chapter 2 will compare volunteering and activism, showing how they are different and asking how they can complement each other. When cut off from one another, both may wither.

In any society, civic associations work in a balance with markets and state. Chapter 3 examines this balance. Common sense in the USA and the UK often says that if the state is strong, civic life is weak, but this chapter will draw on numerous studies to show that our common sense is wrong. It has not been the case in American history, and is not true about the rest of the world, either. Common sense, in places like the USA and UK, holds that a combination of volunteers and the market is the ideal solution to nearly all social problems, whereas in places like Norway or France, common sense holds that the state can do more to provide people with basic rights – to prevent poverty, hunger, and homelessness, to educate children, and to provide resources for aiding the sick and the elderly. Both sorts of countries have active civic associations, but the tripod of "market," "state," and "civic association" balances differently in the different nations.

Chapter 4 examines a prevalent form of civic association: the Non-Governmental Organization (NGO; also called "nonprofit" in the USA). Both volunteering and activism now tend to take place in NGOs. Many NGOs share a set of often mismatched missions: to be open and inclusive; to respect grassroots, local unique people, places, and customs; to encourage innovation, experimentation, and personal transformation among participants; to help the needy; and to provide full, clear, transparent documentation to multiple, distant, hurried donors. Drawing on NGOs' experience in Albania, Malawi, Nigeria, the USA, and elsewhere, this chapter will show that these noble missions often clash. Again, we see that the seemingly harmless aid to the needy can sometimes cause great harm.

Vast inequality is another possible culprit in the quest to find out what hampers healthy civic associations. The wealthy and powerful have almost always participated more in civic affairs than the poor and downtrodden. Lately, wealthy, powerful funders have been creating fake civic associations: "Astroturf" instead of "grassroots" associations. In chapter 5, we have to ask what happens when social inequality becomes so vast that ordinary volunteers or activists become tiny specks compared to these powerful giants. This chapter describes the obstacles that non-elites face when trying to participate.

After all these discouraging chapters, it might be easy to conclude that volunteers and activists are helpless to make the world better. But this would be an incorrect conclusion. Civic associations can and often do change the world for the better. Chapter 6 asks how civic associations try to overcome the difficulties that the previous chapters have described.

Some Provisional Definitions and Two Warnings

We all love to love civic associations. We unquestioningly assume that they promote democracy, freedom, equality, solidarity, fellow-feeling, and reasonableness. Caution! The history of lofty, "keywords" like these – volunteer, democracy, freedom, equality, reason, and the like – has been one of debate, struggle, and war. What one theorist would call free and democratic, another would call forced and undemocratic. When Nation A goes to war against Nation B, each often accuses the other of lacking "democracy." They often mean different things by the term.

Having just said that every definition is a result of a big battle, I will now, before beginning, offer some very provisional definitions that are needed, as starting points – as diving boards from which we will almost immediately bounce away. But when, for example, reporters in the mainstream media use them, the following are the usual definitions they have in mind.

Government

The "government" (also called "the state") is a set of organizations that controls key elements of social reproduction such as the educational system, is recognized by other "states," on the world stage, and has a monopoly on the use of violence in a geographical territory. It can, thus, force people to do what they do not all always want to do – fight in wars, pay taxes, go to school, pay for groceries instead of stealing them. All societies have some means of keeping order, even against some members' wills. A state is one. It does not have to turn an immediate profit the way most businesses do, so it can engage in very long-term projects like highway building. Some examples of state entities are: a local City Council, Congress, the courts, public schools, the National Highway Safety Board, the Department of Child and Family Services, Yosemite National Park.

Economy

The "economy" refers to the exchange of goods and services. Most of the world has a capitalist economy, which means that it is in private hands, run by people who are not elected by the public. The heads of businesses are supposed to make money for themselves and their stockholders. They give, or deny people access to their means of survival – a job. Some corporations have budgets that are bigger than whole nations, and with this money, their leaders can become more powerful in some ways than elected leaders. Their power is different from the power of state officials: CEOs can give you a job, or cut your pay in half, or close up shop, move to Indonesia and leave your city in shambles. Some examples of businesses big and small are: Exxon, the local donut shop, a veterinarian, McDonalds, Apple, a rock band that routinely succeeds in making money selling music, and a rock band that tries to make money selling music but routinely fails.

Civic association, or Non-Governmental Organization (NGO)

Some examples of these are: The Red Cross, Greenpeace, a parent association at the local elementary school, the Ku Klux Klan, a soup kitchen for homeless people, a local astronomy club. What puts these unlikely objects on the same table? It is not that they "do good things," since obviously, no one could agree with all of these organizations. Rather, a civic association is a group of people who voluntarily band together to do something that they think will help their community or the world. When they band together, each individual member hopes to have a say in their group's activities. Members are supposed to leave their inequalities – of class, race, gender, background – at the door. The organization is neither entirely controlled by the government nor a profit-making company, though it may get some funds from such a source. It is not primarily engaged in making money for its members, though it may sell things. A parent association at the elementary school, for example, hosts the Halloween Festival to raise funds for the school. Unlike business leaders, civic organizations' leaders are not supposed to become wealthy by leading an association; if they do, it is a scandal. Civic associations' power is supposed to come not mainly from money or force, but from persuasion and cooperation. By banding together, even if initially over something small, participants might weld themselves into a powerful political force that can influence the course of history.

Democracy

One of this book's themes circles around the connection between "civic participation" and "democracy," so a short definition of democracy is necessary. This is one of the most argued-over words in human history – aside from, say, "God." So we will begin here with only the most minimal definition possible: Democracy is a way of organizing a collectivity – a group or an entire society – in which each member has a say in deciding how the collectivity will proceed.

These definitions are, so far, only the standard ones that one would find implied in a newspaper article. There is another key term that will be used throughout the book, in a way that is not at all standard:

Common sense

In normal conversation, it is good to have "common sense." For social science, however, "common sense" is often a problem. Common sense allows people to make their way through life without too much friction, but as the philosopher Antonio Gramsci pointed out, sometimes, there is a good reason to question the way things are, even if questioning makes you uncomfortable or makes you act in ways that others find inappropriate. For this reason, a Civil Rights Movement song goes,

> It isn't nice to block the doorway,
> It isn't nice to go to jail,
> There are nicer ways to do it,
> But the nice ways always fail.
> It isn't nice . . .
> But if that is Freedom's price
> We don't mind. (Reynolds 1964)

In this book, when you see the phrase "common sense," expect an idea that may seem, at first glance, to be easy and comfortable to use, but may be a sneaky lubrication that allows you to go with the flow, even when the flow includes terrible injustice. In other words, "common sense," in this book, is treated as a problem.

Sorry if all that seemed too remedial! For many students, an obstacle to reading the newspaper is that they are unclear about basic definitions of "government" and "economy." One student at a top university waxed indignant to me that there are Starbucks everywhere, and he called it an example of "big government." Someone else said it was outrageous that "big businesses like the State of Wisconsin" and "Congress" have too much power. Of course, these two students had the terms reversed: in fact, Starbucks is "business," and the state of Wisconsin is part of the larger government.

Saying that each term is actually a constellation of arguments does not mean that the terms are meaningless. People need them as reference points. They are like beacons for ships that do not share a path but at least know where they are, on a shared map. Social theory's job is to clarify our passionately held, unstated assumptions and ideas, discover the roots of competing definitions, and understand what the consequences are of defining them one way or another. So, do not expect to finish this book with single, tidy definitions of equality, freedom, reason, civic, or any other keywords. Instead, you will come away with a map of the warring definitions of "civic association." Depending on how we define good civic participation, we will organize ourselves differently, to do different tasks in our volunteer and activist groups. Millions of people spend billions of hours working in these associations, accomplishing good things and sometimes inadvertently creating disasters. The stakes are high.

1

Why Do Theorists Say Associations Are Crucial for Democracy?

In American society, the volunteer has long been a nearly sacred figure, and the voluntary civic association has been seen as a cure for nearly all social problems. This chapter will describe these hopes. But do not be lulled by this chapter's story of civic association as a cure-all. The rest of the book will describe ways that these cures can go wrong.

The painting overleaf shows a heroic image of the civic participant – if civic engagement were a religion, this painting could be our icon. Why? It gives us an image of ourselves that highlights some of our core ideals: egalitarianism and individualism. The speaker is obviously a worker, with roughened hands and a plain brown jacket, and yet, the suits listen attentively and respectfully. By participating in this meeting, the suits and the plain folks will learn to listen to one another, develop mutual respect and a feeling of fellowship as they work together. They are convinced that their decision will have an effect on something important.

To understand this faith, many superb studies survey its multiple sources in American culture and in Western culture more broadly, but this book will take a different approach. We will pour ourselves inside three key thinkers and see the world through their eyes. I chose these three because they represent very different perspectives on civic engagement's place in society.

Writing in the 1830s and 1840s, Alexis de Tocqueville was amazed at Americans' peppy participation in small, local civic associations that did things like build roads and hospitals. A hundred

Norman Rockwell's *Freedom of Speech* (from the series *Four Freedoms*), 1948.
Norman Rockwell Museum, Stockbridge, MA.

years later, Jane Addams, experiencing the bewildering diversity and sprawling complexity of early twentieth-century Chicago, saw an urgent need for this tradition of civic engagement to continue, but to transform, to address the problems of a society that had changed since Tocqueville's era. Addams' own volunteer work ended up being most effective when she pressured the state, for programs like workplace safety regulations (when there were almost none), sanitation (when garbage pick-up was not routine), playgrounds (she helped invent the concept!), parks, schools, and laws mandating decent wages. At around the same time as Addams, another activist and theorist, Emma Goldman (2006), was writing about workers' self-run businesses in Spain and elsewhere, describing the possibilities for personal and social transformation in them. To her mind, volunteers who meet after-hours, after work, to figure out how to establish garbage pick-ups or parks are missing the point. The main problem, Goldman says, is that most people lack decision-making power when they are at work, and have little control over the economy. Without dramatic changes in the way we earn our daily bread, volunteering, she implies, will always just be a band-aid stuck onto a gaping wound. Here are three very different portraits of civic engagement, focusing on three different corners of a big canvas. Our three authors do have some grounds for agreement: they all insist that people are not born good citizens; they need to learn how to be good, and the forms of association that these writers describe are the informal "schools" for it.

Readers who already are familiar with this map might skim or skip this chapter. The historical background is worth understanding, though, and the arguments continue to this day, though, so we begin with Tocqueville.

The Iconic Figure and Tocquevillean Volunteering

Tocqueville's story about "America" is partly an historical observation and partly a projection of his own hopes and fears. Tocqueville, who came from an aristocratic French family, was both intrigued and terrified by the idea of democracy, but saw that this idea was gathering momentum, poised to take over the earth. From his voyage to America, he concluded that without grassroots civic associations democracy would collapse, and a disorganized, fearful, lonely, hot-headed, small-minded, and mean-spirited population would rule.

Tocqueville has a practical agenda here, not just a theory. He is interested in stacking luck's deck, so that no matter what innate intelligence or generosity people have at birth, social conditions can sway the game. He has very little faith in people's innate decency. People are not born good citizens or bad citizens, good or bad people, caring or uncaring, selfish or altruistic, greedy or generous, passive or active, Tocqueville says. Their societies train them to be good or bad, in very small, constant, steady, everyday ways: the steady constant drip drip drip that creates canyons and valleys, not a big, one-time splash. "Common sense" tells us that good people create a good society, but Tocqueville reverses the arrows: a good society creates good individuals. Intuitively, this makes sense: a decent society is more likely to produce decent individuals than a war-like, mean-spirited, vicious society is. In saying this, he could be dubbed the world's first sociologist, when he asserted over and over that there is nothing that can clearly be called "human nature" except for our amazing ability to be so incredibly *different* in different societies.

Tocqueville goes further than this obvious intuition, by specify-ing the mechanisms that create good or bad people and societies. He says that in *democracies*, civic associations both make individ-uals better and improve society as a whole. What is so potentially terrifying and potentially inspiring about Tocqueville's story about democracies is that he says that creating good citizens who are capable of good self-rule requires a *whole way of life*, not just a civics class in high school or a vote every four years. He says that participating in associations offers people cognitive, emotional, and political benefits.

Knowledge – cognitive benefits:

Participants develop decision-making skills, skills in creating an organization, and knowledge about how organizations operate.

Society benefits. In associations, people conduct open-ended discussions about political issues. Informal deliberation helps them think up better solutions than they would if they were just thinking all by themselves.

Solidarity – emotional benefits:

Participants develop fellow feeling for one another. They learn to take each others' interests into account, to keep asking, "what's good for society as a whole?" and to compromise. Society benefits. Associations can develop support networks for anyone who becomes needy.

Power – political benefits:

Participants learn how to make real changes. Society benefits. Everyone, not just elites, will have a say in decisions about public issues.

So What Could Possibly Go Wrong with Democracy?

Isn't "democracy" just another word for "good?" According to Tocqueville, no. After portraying this wholesome, uncontroversial image of democracy, he goes on to a terrifying image of democracy gone awry. His worry is this: what if democracy puts government in the hands of majority *without* constantly training that majority in the arts of self-governance? He gives many good reasons to expect this disaster in democracies, and says that civic associations can prevent most of them.

Fear of attachment and fear of dependence

First, Tocqueville is worried that people in democracies will forget how deeply they depend on one another. For most of the previous thousand years, Europeans had been linked together in a hierarchy, bound in a system of mutual obligation that linked nobles to peasants. Peasants enjoyed many customary rights that made their survival possible: to gather firewood and hunt deer in the nobles' forests; to graze sheep on the nobles' land; to be protected, by nobles, from invasion; to be helped by nobles in times of famine and illness (Hobsbawm 1962). Everyone had a set place and a set of customary duties. A long chain of mutual obligation attached rich to poor, parent to child to grandchild, brother to sister, bishop to parishioner, noble to layman. He says, "Aristocracy links everyone, from peasant to king, in one long chain. Democracy breaks the chain and frees each link" (Tocqueville 1968: 508).

This simple couplet evokes a ghost that has been haunting democracies for centuries: if people no longer imagine a solid hierarchy linking all humans to each other, inside a larger "Great Chain of Being," as medieval Europeans called it, linking angels and deities to humans, on down to worms and fish, nothing would prevent the rich from treating the poor like trash. Without this chain linking everyone and everything together, the universe starts to seem like a warehouse full of spare parts. People who live in most traditional societies are, Tocqueville said, anchored to each other and to the land, whereas "Americans" – who stand in for his somewhat abstract model of "people in a democracy" – frantically dash from one place to another, never settling down long enough to establish deep connections, always striving for something better before they have had time to enjoy what they already have. Such people could just use each other, and society could become a big machine that spit people out when they were used up.

After democracies break these rigid, secure, built-in attachments up and down the hierarchy, people might just imagine themselves as totally detached from one another, as if they held their entire fate in their own hands.

> Such folk [people in a democracy, as opposed to an aristocracy] owe no man anything and hardly expect anything from anybody. They form the habit of thinking of themselves in isolation and imagine that their whole destiny is in their own hands. (Tocqueville 1968: 508)

This is a big peril to democracy, says Tocqueville. Like the good proto-sociologist that he was, he says that this belief, that one can cut oneself off from society and be completely self-sufficient, is simply incorrect. He urgently repeats, over and over, that no one can live outside of the web of relationships. People need each other, not just for material goods, but also for a sense of self, and an emotionally coherent life. Imagining that you can cut yourself out of the web simply prevents you from understanding yourself, he says. To understand your real, everyday life conditions is inseparable from understanding who you are.

Some Americans still imagine that they could survive on their own, without any help from "outsiders" like the government, even though we all know, realistically, that even our water comes from hundreds of miles away. Some websites and books, for example, teach people about "living off the grid." Tocqueville, were he reborn today, might wryly observe that they were written on computers that were probably made in China, while the writers were eating Costa Rican bananas, and drinking water that was not poisonous because the government prevented a factory upstream from polluting it. When people stop acknowledging their inevitable connection to one another, they stop making sure that their world is livable together, and democracy vanishes.

What can prevent this first peril from taking hold? Civic associations come to the rescue! Making decisions in local associations gives ordinary people a vision of the big picture, showing them how they are inevitably part of a great chain. But here, in democracies as opposed to other societies, making the "chain" is supposed to be conscious, and each individual is supposed to have a voice and a choice. Local civic associations bring decision-making down to the reach of the average, unexceptional person – even someone who does not have a special fondness for political affairs.

It is difficult to force a man out of himself and get him to take an interest in the affairs of the whole state, for he has little understanding of the way in which the fate of the state can influence his own lot. But if it is a question of taking a road past his property, he sees at once that this small public matter has a bearing on his greatest private interests,

and there is no need to point out to him the close connection between
his private profit and the general interest.
[but a direct translation of the end from the original French is: "...
and he will discover, without anyone's showing him, the tight connection between his particular interest and the general interest."]
(Tocqueville 1961: 150–1, my translation)

When this fellow joins the association to decide where to build
the highway, he bridges a gap between personal experience and
politics. He will understand how he depends on other people.
Participating in local decision-making, in a civic association, will
also prove to him the value of cooperation. Whereas democratic
societies tend to give people the false impression that they are
entirely independent of one another, working together in associations shows them how much more effective they are when they
work together. It would be silly, for example, if the highway only
went in front of this individual's house, but then ended a block
later. This fellow might learn to compromise, to say "We will start
by paving ten streets across town first, and then start paving the
street near my house when we've finished." This was what participants in a "participatory budget" process decided, in a Brazilian
city in the early 2000s (Baiocchi 2002). (We will come back to this
in chapter 6.) Participants learned that a rising tide raises all boats.
This is Tocqueville's concept of "self-interest rightly understood."
If the man with the highway were alive today, he might support
environmental protection so that he could have clean water, even
if it means that he could not dump his own sewage in the nearby
river. It is not heroic, not even really altruism, but a simple recognition that always fighting for one's own immediate interests is
often self-defeating.

Tyranny of the majority

When democracy "breaks the chain and frees each link," a second
potential peril to democracy arises: it is hard for citizens to learn
how to link themselves back together. Instead of joining in open-
ended, reasonable associations, they might form a "tyranny of

the majority." Each link, in this metaphor, is like a speck of flour, blowing whichever way the wind blows; with just a drop of water, the little specks of flour might glue themselves together too tightly and massify (Tocqueville 1968: 433). Mob rule, witch hunts, and fanaticism set in.

A "tyranny of the majority" is more potent than a monarch's power. A king's power is centralized in one place, but a lot can go on behind the king's back. In a democracy, in contrast, ". . . all the parties are ready to recognize the rights of the majority because they all hope one day to profit themselves by them" (Tocqueville 1968: 248). Each individual is a "ruler" of sorts. Eyes are everywhere. In contrast, ". . . no monarch is so absolute that he can hold all the forces of society in his hands, and overcome all resistance, as a majority invested with the right to make the laws and to execute them" (Tocqueville 1968: 254). If a person in a democracy disagrees with the majority's opinions, where can he or she turn? There are no other powers to which to turn; there is almost nothing outside of the majority.

Imagine the person who does not agree with the majority, or can't conform. If a "tyranny of the majority" develops, the whole society turns into one interminable seventh-grade class in the 1950s, before there were rules against harassment, and you are the gay thirteen-year-old who thinks you are the only one of his kind on the planet. "When once its mind is made up on any question, there are . . . no obstacles which can retard, much less halt, its progress and give it time to hear the wails of those it crushes as it passes" (Tocqueville 1968: 248). In such conditions, democracy vanishes.

Civic associations to the rescue, again! Where there are plural civic associations, Tocqueville implies, people learn to tolerate opposing views, even if they do not agree with them. For example, there are, in contrast to the 1950s, now civic associations that defend gay rights, so the specks of flour cannot turn into a hard lump and crush their opponents quite as easily. There *is* somewhere else to turn.

Tocqueville considers this to be one of the most important things that democracy does: protect a space for private decision-making.

In his day, the decisions that thinkers like him wanted to make private were about religion, so that the religious wars of his era would end. Now we can add sexuality, and a whole host of other freedoms. Often, we protect them with voluntary associations, as the gay rights example illustrates. And then, they become topics of debate, regarding just how private they really should be. Your child-raising practices generally are nobody's business but your own, but if they include abuse, they are someone else's business, for example. We all can publicly debate the possibility of leaving decisions in private hands. This isn't possible in places that have no associations to conduct the argument. Participating in associations can, in Tocqueville's mind, prevent people from becoming so hot-headed and passionate, they kill each other over minor, or even major, differences. A person in a civic association will, says Tocqueville, learn to protect spaces for private decision-making, not just for him or herself, but for everyone.

Limitlessness and the infinite, constant need to prove one's worthiness

A third peril arises in democracies: overly fierce competition. This is a byproduct of democracy's promise of equality, Tocqueville says. Before going on to his logic here, we need to know that by "equality," Tocqueville does not mean that everyone will be the same. As he points out, some people are smarter, swifter, more musical, or better at math than others. Differences between individuals are inevitable. Rather, by "equality," he means that people can potentially move up the social ladder, and potentially make their voices heard, and potentially change their society as well.

Ironically, however, the promise of equality poses a third peril to good citizenship, Tocqueville argues. Unlike people in previous societies, where people have stable, though unequal, social positions, people in democracies are supposed to be equals, but know they are not. The result can be a frenzied, frantic quest to appear to be first among equals, to prove your worthiness to yourself by grabbing at whatever is new, always hurrying, never satisfied, never still.

"Democratic institutions awaken and flatter the passion for equality without being able to satisfy it entirely. This complete equality is always slipping through the people's fingers at the moment when they think to grasp it." The promise of equality can make people so competitive, they "never stop thinking of the good things they have not got . . . clutch at everything but hold nothing fast, and so lose grip as they hurry after some new delight . . ." (Tocqueville 1968: 536).

This may resemble what we now call consumerism, but it is not about savoring material delights. On the contrary, it is about proving to yourself that you are a worthy person, and never being able to settle down long enough to appreciate anything before rushing on. If citizens are too nervously and busily scurrying after the next fleeting status marker, they might stop taking care of their society. They may welcome a ruler who will just seize power and make all the decisions without asking for them to take time away from their constant pursuit. Democracy would vanish.

Civic associations could come to the rescue again! In associations, people learn to cooperate, and they see the results of cooperation, when they build schools and roads and solve social problems together. Working together in associations gives people a way to prove their worthiness to themselves in a way that potentially benefits everyone.

It is important to note here that Tocqueville was very much in favor of *moderate* competition in the economy. He said that people in democracies, unlike people in aristocracies, honor and respect hard work. Comparing the slave states of the South with the free states of the North, he sees that equality in the North makes the farmers work harder. Every square inch of land is lovingly tended in the North because the farmers know that they will profit from whatever productivity they can squeeze from their rocky soil, whereas in the South, the slaves do as little as they can, because they will not benefit by working harder. Forcing the slaves to work takes work itself. Someone has to force the slaves to work in the South, but nobody has to force the independent farmers in the North to work, because they want to work, to compete. In the North, this delicate balance of equality and competition works because competition is moderate, not excessive. We will come back to this point in chapter 3.

"Aristocracy of industry" – concentration of the economy in fewer and fewer hands

In a society that allows people to feel so detached, a fourth specter haunts democracy: the heads of industry could become too powerful, and economic power too concentrated in too few hands. If the gap between rich and poor becomes too vast, the people who run big businesses will become like aristocrats who command vast empires. He calls this class an "aristocracy of industry." If an aristocracy of industry arises, democracy vanishes, for two reasons.

The first is that the wealthy and powerful will gain practice, every day, in making big decisions, when they make big decisions all day long. The workers, in contrast, will become more and more like animals that repeat the same motion all day, and have no chance to make decisions while they are at work.

> While the workman confines his intelligence more and more to studying one single detail, the master daily embraces a vast field in his vision, and his mind expands as fast as the other's contracts. Soon the latter will need no more than bodily strength, without intelligence . . . The former becomes more and more like the administrator of a huge empire, and the latter more like a brute. (Tocqueville 1968: 556)

What shocks Tocqueville most is the possibility that the people at the top could just throw workers in the trash when they get old or injured, or business is slow. When democracy breaks the chain and frees each link, employers have no obligation to workers. The workers become things to them, not people. This is the second reason that concentration of control of production in the hands of a tiny minority is unhealthful for democracy. It creates a situation that is as unequal and hierarchical as an aristocracy, but without the customary chain of responsibility that linked rich to poor. Tocqueville calls such conditions "monstrous."

The territorial aristocracy of past ages was obliged by law, or thought itself obliged by custom, to come to the help of its servants and relieve their distress. But the industrial aristocracy of our day, when it has impoverished and brutalized the men it uses, abandons them in time of crisis, to public charity to feed them. (Tocqueville 1968: 515–16)

In such conditions, democracy vanishes.

Civic associations *don't* come to the rescue! There is not much in Tocqueville's theory that could prevent the "aristocracy of industry" from developing. He considered the possibility of workers' forming associations to protect themselves, but decided that such unions would fail because workers would always be too poor to provide mutual aid (583–4). Beyond this, there would have to be some other cross-class civic association, in which elites and lowly people alike participated in a way that made elites feel solidarity with their subordinates. As we will see later in this book, though, despite the iconic painting, multiclass civic associations are the exception, not the rule.

Government centralization

A fifth danger to democracy is that the *government* might become too centralized and powerful. Before describing this fifth peril, we need to see that Tocqueville's theory ranges from what would now be called a "Right-wing critique" to a "Left-wing critique," to "neither." Part of what everyone loves about Tocqueville is that almost anyone can pick through his writings and find what they agree with in them: The Left quotes him to condemn an economy that is too concentrated in too few hands at the top, while the Right quotes him to condemn a government that is too powerful.

"Right" and "Left" are, for many Americans, confusing terms, so short definitions are in order. When a political party or movement is "on the Right," it means that it is mainly worried about "big government" and is either not worried about inequality or sees it as an inevitable and even desirable element of a competitive society. The presence of inequality shows, to some Right-wing thinkers, that people who work hard and are very clever reap well-deserved rewards. People on the Right worry more that government experts, in contrast, are too far away and bureaucratic to know how to run anything.

The image of the "aristocracy of industry," on the other hand, shows the "Leftist" side of Tocqueville. When a political party or movement is "on the Left," it usually means that it is mainly worried about inequality, and about unelected big business leaders' control over life, as they try to turn too much of life – education, nature, leisure, water, health care – into a commodity from which they can make money. For this side of Tocqueville, the fear is that workers will become unable to participate as equals in governance, and power will concentrate in too few heads of the economy. While the Right is afraid of government bureaucracy, people on the Left point out that corporations are bureaucracies, too. If the "aristocracy of industry" argument is Tocqueville's Leftist side, the fifth danger, of "centralized government," is the "Right-wing" side of Tocqueville.

For the "Right-wing" side of Tocqueville, government robs people of the creative freedom to pursue their own projects – be they profit-making projects or homespun associations aimed at local improvement. Tocqueville is worried that if the government becomes too powerful, we might stop seeing the need to form local associations:

> It is easy to see the time coming in which men will be less and less able to produce, by each alone, the commonest bare necessities of life. The tasks of government must therefore perpetually increase, and its efforts to cope with them must spread its net ever wider. The more government takes the place of associations, the more will individuals lose the idea of forming associations and need the government to come to their help. That is a vicious circle. And if ultimately, as a result of the minute subdivision of landed property, the land itself is so infinitely parceled out that it can only be cultivated by associations of laborers, must the public administration cope with every industrial undertaking beyond the competence of one individual citizen? ... must the head of the government leave the helm of state to guide the plow? (Tocqueville 1968: 515)

22

In such conditions, democracy vanishes.

Civic associations to the rescue again! Tocqueville would say that centralized decision-making will be less likely to arise as long as this fellow keeps going to meetings to decide about local affairs like the highway. As long as the local people are strong and vigilant in steering their own affairs, the government will not be able to take over local decision-making.

Of course, Tocqueville was talking about a society in which small farmers owned and cultivated their own plots. Now, giant agri-business companies control most farms in the USA, and the people who work the land are poorly paid farm workers. A critique that pointed to an "aristocracy of industry" would probably be more fitting. On the other hand, the US government subsidizes these giant agri-businesses, so if we want to continue his "hand" and "plow" metaphor, we would have to say that the hands of the state are putting money into the hands of the agri-businesses that, in turn, guide the plow. So, right now, we can see that the two problems of an "aristocracy of industry" and "government centralization" work synergistically to make democracy even further from reach than Tocqueville could have imagined. Much more has changed since Tocqueville's era, as we will see in later chapters.

Summary of Tocqueville: Civic Associations to the Rescue!

Civic associations are more necessary in democracies than in other societies, to divert these overwhelming currents, Tocqueville says. Voluntary associations, he says, give people a chance to experience a kind of pleasure that no one else in history has felt before: the pleasure of being the rulers of their own lives together, and of joining together voluntarily, rather than through rote habit or coercion. When ordinary people make decisions together in their small, local, face-to-face groups, they have a chance to be smarter and more powerfully benevolent than anyone in a non-democratic country could dream of being. Not only this: they have joined together voluntarily, on purpose, not because they were thrown together by habit or force. Coordinating society consciously and voluntarily is, he says, its own joy. Participation cultivates a kind of person that can easily do good deeds without having to be royalty to do so. The participant does not have to make dramatic sacrifices, but only be ordinarily decent in an everyday way. But Tocqueville's vision of democracy is like a precarious stool whose legs have to be in near perfect balance or the whole thing will tip over and crash.

Despite huge changes since Tocqueville's era – which will be a major topic of the rest of the book – Tocqueville's iconic image of the nearly sacred volunteer who can do no wrong is the ideal that we carry to this day. Contemporary thinkers and policy-makers have used Tocqueville's ideas (or distorted them) to advocate for small, face-to-face associations. An influential thinker, Robert Putnam, for example, cites Tocqueville to argue that volunteering promotes democracy. So far, so good. But then, citing Putnam's work, policy-makers have funded face-to-face volunteering, while simultaneously advocating cutbacks in social services on the assumption that volunteers should do the job of helping the elderly or the disabled, and that they can do the job in a way that will promote democracy better than trained social service workers can. Following one strand of Tocqueville's thought, they imagine that when the state steps in, volunteers recede. They imagine a see-saw. Whether part-time volunteers can bear the responsibility of running full-time social services is a question that many of these policy-makers seem not to have considered, according to these pol-icies' critics (http://www.bbc.co.uk/news/uk-politics-12092740). We will come back to these questions later. The point is that when we answer the question "How should we think about civic asso-ciations' place in society?" the stakes are high. As we will now see, another powerful strain of thought and action has seriously dis-puted this see-saw relationship between volunteering and the state.

Jane Addams, "Perplexity", and Political Activism

Writing in the early 1900s, Jane Addams was confronting a different society from the one Tocqueville saw. Tocqueville described a *model* of democracy, using illustrations drawn from the real society he visited. For example, he did not count the South as part of American democracy, did not notice women's non-citizenship, and did not mention indentured servants. Addams, in contrast, spent a lifetime as a volunteer in Chicago, and includes all the messy elements that did not fit Tocqueville's useful but fanciful, imaginative model.

Chicago in the early 1900s was like today's Los Angeles, London, Toronto, or, well, Chicago: people from all corners of the planet pouring in, sharing no primordial roots or ancestors, no religious or ethnic heritage, maybe not even a language. There was vast inequality between classes, as well as between members of different races and ethnicities. While this may be exciting and mind-opening, it also poses challenges to people who want to work together and related to one another as themselves as members of one unified society, with a shared fate.

The daughter of a senator, Addams grew up in rural Illinois, far from the multilingual bustle and chaos of Chicago. A girl of her background typically finished off her education with a group voyage through Europe. Her touristic pass takes her not just to Europe's great cathedrals and museums, but also, by happenstance, through the terrible slums of late nineteenth-century London. She is plagued by the idea that her whole experience is only for the seemingly endless "preparation" that occupies youth for so many years, both then and now. This life seems to her to have no socially useful purpose, and the voyage leaves her feeling helpless and useless. Urgently, she needs to escape the tiny bubble in which elite girls like her live. She has a mental breakdown. Crawling out of this claustrophobia-inducing little world of privileged girls, she convinces a friend to go in with her in buying a run-down house near the putrid smelling slaughterhouses of Chicago, where impoverished immigrants live. Together, they set out to improve the lives of America's slum dwellers.

The rambling building, named Hull House, starts as a community center for immigrants to come for discussion groups, English language lessons, music lessons, cooking classes, for help with infants, domestic violence, mental illness, and alcoholism problems. There is a kindergarten for little children, after-school activities for older children, and activities for seniors who are too old to work at paid jobs. By the middle of the twentieth century, there are hundreds of "settlement houses" like Hull House all over the country.

The tales she tells in her autobiography, *Twenty Years at Hull-House,* do not describe what one might suspect of a daughter of a senator who set out to help the poor immigrants. She does not condescend to help "the poor dears," and make them just like her (Daniels 1988); no, she does not simply try to make the immigrants adjust to the status quo. Her idea of civic engagement demands throwing oneself into situations that leave one "perplexed." When she walks in the shoes of the poor, Addams realizes that to be effective, her charitable volunteering has to connect to political activism.

Let us take these revelations one at time: her realization of the need for "perplexity," and her arriving at the idea that effective volunteering to help the needy is not separate from political activism. Together, they pose a challenge to Tocqueville's image of harmonious, easy, apolitical volunteering. As the rest of the book will show, both forms of civic engagement have their respective proponents.

Perplexity

Addams says that in a diverse, inegalitarian, potentially fragmented society, it is your moral duty to put yourself in situations that will make you feel "perplexed:" to get out of your safe, comfortable bubble, in order to challenge and transform your most dearly held assumptions about how to be a good person. In one essay, she portrays "the charity visitor," a young woman who has never had to work, with clean hands and clean clothes. The people she tries to help, in contrast, are dirty and tired. She feels a twinge of superiority, and quickly realizes the mistake:

> The daintily clad charity visitor who steps into the little house . . .
> is no longer sure of her superiority to the latter; she recognizes that
> her hostess after all represents social value and industrial use, as over
> against her own parasitic cleanliness and social standing attained only
> through status. (Addams 2002: 12).

Of course, *she was*, when she had first started volunteering, the
charity visitor, and her shame fairly drips off the page here. She
realizes that the only way for her to start helping these people is
for her to live their lives from the inside, not to apply her ethics
to their lives as if ethics are universal. In fact, she realizes that in a
complex, divided society, any one person's view is too partial to be
a good basis for morality. Therefore, one person's version of being
"good" might end up with dreadfully wrong consequences. Take,
for example, her initial judgment of parents who have to choose
between going homeless and sending their children out to work for
pay when they are young teens. Her first thought is that the family
should make the children go to work, but then she realizes that the
whole situation is wrong.

The initial righteous judgment liquefies; now, she realizes that
her high-minded judgment was, itself, unethical. Someone like
her from her background can go through life without having to
confront this basic wrongness of the whole social arrangement.
Shocked, she realizes that how her world works is not how their
world works. For this family, not letting the young teens find paid
work would mean risking homelessness, separation of parents
from children, and brothers from sisters. Other scenarios involv-
ing the charity visitor show the same pattern: a poor man wants
to be a writer, but she encourages him to write trashy pulp novels,
shunning his ambitions. The charity visitor says to herself that if
he were her friend's husband, from her wealthy background, she
would advise him to follow his star and write serious fiction. But
for the poor man, this choice would be immoral; it would mean
letting his wife and children starve for a while. Again, she realizes
that the only way to resolve this moral dilemma is to see that the
whole situation is wrong. She realizes that the problem is not that
the would-be novelist has chosen one or the other, but that both

options are wrong, that the society has not allowed for any good choices for this man.

> Of course there was always present the harrowing consciousness of the difference in economic condition between ourselves and our neighbors. Even if we had gone to live in the most wretched tenement, there would have always been an essential difference between them and ourselves, for we should have had a sense of security in regard to illness and old age and the lack of these two securities are the specters which most persistently haunt the poor. (Addams 1960 [1910]: 134–5)

From all of this, she concludes that the only ethical mode of living in a diverse and inegalitarian society is to throw yourself into situations that force you to question your most basic assumptions about how the world works – to question the ground while you are walking on it.

> Already we are under a moral obligation in choosing our experiences, since the result of those experiences must ultimately determine our understanding of our life. We know instinctively that if we grow contemptuous of our fellows, and consciously limit our intercourse to certain kinds of people whom we have previously decided to respect, we not only tremendously circumscribe our range of life, but limit the scope of our ethics. (Addams 2002: 8)

Curiosity, for her, is a drive, which is simultaneously emotional, moral, and intellectual. Without curiosity, a person is trapped in a little bubble, inconsiderate, and ignorant. No matter how high minded such a person is, his or her principles will always be partial and immoral.

This may, on the face of it, sound like many summer and spring break programs' high-flown rhetoric about how volunteering should be "emotionally transformative." One such program, for example, invites participants to walk in immigrants' shoes, to experience the desert border crossing between Mexico and the USA. But usually, when study-abroad programs and other nonprofit volunteer program advertise that they will be "transformative," they mean something much less upsetting and much more short-term and easy than what Addams described. The program that invites participants to walk in the immigrants' shoes lasts only for two weeks, with plenty of water and a jeep full of supplies following in case they get tired or thirsty (Adler 2012).

A bridge to political activism

From her decades at Hull House, Addams realized that if she were serious about wanting to help the poor, she had to link their local, immediate concerns – for health care, elder care, safe streets, for example – all the way "up" to city, state, and national political activism. Take the example of the family that sends its children out to make money. Her initial shock gives way to empathy with the parents, when she sees that homelessness is hovering close by as a likely alternative for this family. But can she leave it at that, just shrug her shoulders and say that in cases of poverty, child labor is really okay? Or should she just give money to this one family and hope that there is another Jane Addams who will give money to another family in similarly desperate conditions?

No, she decides that the only solution is to change the conditions that make poor people take such desperate measures – to make companies pay the parents enough so that the kids do not have to go to work. Can she just help this one family and then go home, well satisfied with her achievement? Obviously, helping them is better than not helping them, but not enough, for her. Rather, her mission is to change the conditions, to make poverty less brutal, for all families, even families whose members are not very clever, healthy, strong, or good at turning a profit.

This may sound like socialism. Perhaps in a very mild form, it is. In a capitalist economy, working people have to sell themselves or starve. They have to sell themselves just like any other commodity, but they are still not quite the same as washing machines. Unlike other commodities, the humans cannot sit in a warehouse for a few years if there is a slump in demand for labor, or if they are not as smart or healthy as their neighbor. All Addams wanted (in Gøsta Esping-Anderson words, 1990) was laws that would "de-commodify" people enough to protect them from the most deadly ravages of poverty.

So, her charitable efforts force her into a wider political world. An example from *Twenty Years at Hull House* involves animal corpses. What if the owners of the slaughterhouses drop off dead animals on unpaved ghetto streets, where they sink into the mud and sicken children while the parents are at work? Her answer is not just to tell the parents personally to keep each individual child away, or to move to a neighborhood with paved streets and fewer corpses. This would be an individual solution, but would not fix the problem for children whose parents did not leave. Addams' initial answer is to fix the problem locally with a small incinerator that the local folks build. Here is a perfect Tocquevillean solution!

However, she soon realizes that she needs more than volunteer work. Tocqueville is not enough. Rather, Hull House has to put pressure on the city to pave the streets and to establish routine garbage pick-up.

> ... although a woman may sweep her own doorway in her native village [in Italy] and allow the refuse to innocently decay in the open air and sunshine, in a crowded city quarter [in Chicago], if the garbage is not properly collected and destroyed, a tenement-house mother may see her children sicken and die, and that the immigrants must therefore not only keep their own houses clean, but must also help the authorities to keep the city clean. (Addams 2002 [1901])

She has, in other words, arrived at a political solution. Here is another example of her way of linking volunteering and political activism: Are teenagers wandering the street with nothing to do but make trouble? Do not just call an evening curfew, but give them something wholesome to do – thus, she joins with other civic leaders to initiate the first playgrounds in the USA (Addams 2005 [1909]; McArthur 1975; Skocpol 1995).

She and her fellow settlement house workers connected volunteering and politics in these ways. Their political solutions worked on multiple fronts to make the pains of poverty less severe. One was to press for child labor to be outlawed, while simultaneously pressing the government to establish minimum wage laws for adult workers, so that parents' jobs can support a family. This way, employers can live up to their own morals, so this solution is good for the families as well as the employers: If employers have to compete against each other, they cannot live up to their own morals. To keep their firm afloat, they have to compete with other employers to produce an ever-cheaper product. It becomes too tempting to pay workers starvation wages. When Addams fights to make it illegal to pay starvation wages, she allows employers – both the benevolent and the wicked ones – to avoid this race to the bottom. Protecting the employers from this aspect of market competition gives the employers a chance to live in a society that *makes it easier to be good.*

Another front on which she works is to pressure the government to make sure that workplaces are not so dangerous, a desperate parent will not be *allowed* to accept a job that risks life and limb. So if previous workers at a job site have lost fingers or limbs, even the worker who is desperate or foolish enough to want the job will not be able to take it.

People like Addams, and their fellow activists in labor unions, won these battles. Therefore, there were relatively strong laws about these issues in the mid twentieth century in the USA and other wealthy nations. However, the fight has re-opened. Critics of policies like the ones she won say that state control over people's free choice is wrong. They call controls like these examples of "a nanny state." If we want to revoke these laws and make regulation voluntary, we would have to agree that when that second worker steps in to the dangerous job site, either in ignorance or desperation, it should be considered the second worker's own problem.

Comparison with Tocqueville

Addams argued that civic engagement aiming to help those who can't help themselves often requires state action, for example, regulation of the stockyards to make sure there are rules about dumping dead animal on unpaved streets, for garbage pickup, for workplace safety laws, for playgrounds, parks, minimum wage laws, and more. Just as importantly, she wanted to make sure that these regulations were enforced, by many government workers who check. Again, this may sound, to the Right-wing critics, perilously close to "big government."

If we go back to Tocqueville's precarious balancing act, we can see that Addams might retort that sometimes, creating a powerful *government* (one of Tocqueville's "perils" to democracy) is the only way to prevent the harms that come from an *economy* that is too concentrated in too few hands (another of his "perils"). If powerful businesses want to dump dead cows on the streets, no one can stop them except a powerful government. In the case of dead cows, the risk of "big government" is, to Addams' mind, not as dangerous as the risk of big business.

Addams often implied that she was updating ideas like Tocqueville's, adjusting them to life in a class-divided, industrial metropolis. Over and over, she says that the solutions that worked for rural folks would not work in big cities. Throwing the garbage outside and waiting for it to decompose or be eaten by birds, or sending the children out to work in healthful sunlight, picking oranges and playing in the groves, might be fine in rural Italy, where many of Hull House's participants came from. But in a big, dense, dirty city, just letting things happen naturally like that was not an option. The little incinerator for the big dead animals – a nice do-it-yourself solution – was not enough. Between Tocqueville's day and Addams' day, the American landscape had transformed. Have we adjusted to this transformation yet? Or do we still imagine ourselves to be heroically "living off the grid," along with all the self-sufficiency and separateness that we imagine accompanying it? We will return to this question in chapter 3, to ask how and when hands-on, one-on-one civic volunteering is the best solution, and how and when it is not. Along with Addams, people in many nations have decided that sometimes, establishing laws and a stronger state to enforce them is a better solution.

Another big difference between Addams and Tocqueville concerns how much extraordinary work volunteering takes. Tocqueville's citizens are ordinary people. That is the beauty of his image: anyone can do it, without any heroic effort or creativity. His image is of "the strength of weak ties" (Granovetter 1973), a thin web that extends over nearly the entire society, almost unbeknownst to the people who are lured into cultivating those weak ties.

Addams also puts more stock in the *state* to create conditions in which employers are not forced to engage in a self-destructive "race to the bottom" and workers are paid enough to survive in decency. So, in one way, her image of a good society requires less individual work than Tocqueville's. But, in another way, her image requires more risk-taking. Within this somewhat safe social framework, her "charity visitor" takes great moral, emotional risks. This character is a brave, imaginative person, willing to turn herself inside-out, to inspect her most basic presuppositions, to question the very grounds on which she walks. Such a person will not rest complacent in a tightly constricted, class-segregated bubble. She will recognize that throwing herself into situations of "perplexity" is the only route to realistic morality in a world that is brimming over with confusing, multiple forms of life.

Emma Goldman and Workers' Collectives

Rather than limiting itself to after-hours volunteer work, civic engagement can start in the place where most people have to spend the biggest portion of their waking hours: work. This form of civic association is called "workplace democracy." Other names for this form of engagement are "social enterprises," "workers' cooperatives," or "workers' collectives." They are not all exactly the same thing, but what these organizations all share is that the employees make decisions, without having a boss at the top who collects the money, and everyone who works in the place has a significant voice in the decisions the organization makes. This form of civic life makes the *workplace* into a place that operates the way Tocqueville imagined civic associations operating, as a setting in which people learn to make decisions together for the good of all, and in which they develop the power to enforce their decisions. Goldman is not as fond of state solutions as Addams is; Goldman assumes that when the workplace itself becomes a place where average people can make important decisions about their daily lives, the state will become less and less necessary.

What is workplace democracy? Advocates of workplace democracy want all the employees in a firm to have the power to decide what to produce, how much to produce, how much to reinvest, how to improve production, how many hours a day to work: in short, all the decisions about production that executives normally make. The idea is to make the workplace itself into a kind of "civic" association: the employees will get to practice democratic decision-making while they are at work. They get to decide how to make decisions for the good of the collectivity. In this way, they make "work," which is usually, in the standard, "common sense" definition, considered an "economic" activity, also into a *civic* activity.

Around the world, we can find a workers cooperative, or collective, providing just about every good or service imaginable. A network of such firms in the San Francisco Bay Area is called the Network of Bay Area Workers Cooperatives. Its acronym NoBawc, is pronounced No boss! The pronunciation is apt. These kinds of organizations are a significant part of the economy in some places. In 2004, the Canadian government started a fund to promote "social enterprise" (Laville, Levesque, and Mendell 2006). Some of these workers' self-managed firms are market enterprises, such as natural food coops and recycling businesses (or, in the San Francisco case, a coop strip joint!). Others involved more voluntary labor, or exclusively voluntary labor, such as parent day care cooperative, in which each family might be responsible to watch the children one day per week. In the mid 1980s, over half of the children in England and Wales who were in day care were in such a program (Laville, Levesque, and Mendell 2006). Similar enterprises exist all over Europe in various forms, employing several million people all together. Within the USA, the cooperative, or social enterprise, movement is small. In various parts of the country, there is a long history of cooperatives. During the era of the family farm, dairy farmers in the Midwest pooled their resources to store their milk, make cheese and butter, and ship their goods. Now, there are, according to one survey, 30,000 cooperatives in the USA, employing more than two million people

(Hightower 2012). The region Emma Goldman studied has now become one of the largest networks of cooperatives in the world. The Mondragon cooperative network of northern Spain now includes companies in every inhabited continent, producing everything from machine parts to waste-water treatment plants to furniture.

Of course, one would need to do a very thorough study to decide how fully they all live up to the democratic vision of Mondragon's founders (Whyte and Whyte 1991). And even if they did, some scholars and activists worry that this kind of activism can make political activists less vocal; they get preoccupied with figuring out different ways of storing flour in the coop grocery store, or keeping cats out of the pre-school's sandbox, and might stop protesting about bigger issues. On the other hand, it makes activism more of an everyday affair, diffused throughout the day.

Goldman's descriptions of a network of such enterprises in 1930s Spain are especially vivid and concrete. Goldman focused on grape and dairy farms; for a contemporary account of a similar firm, one can read the detailed transcripts of a grocery store collective's meetings in Madison, Wisconsin (Gastil 1993). Both show that these organizations spend a great deal of time talking about what to do. They both show a division of labor, so someone who is very good at bookkeeping might do that, while someone who is good at woodworking might focus on that, but they also show that everyone makes important decisions about the enterprise as a whole. Surprisingly – perhaps implausibly? – in Goldman's stories, laziness is not a problem. When given the chance, the people she observed preferred to have more control over their lives than less, even if that meant going to meetings and working as hard as they collectively decided to work. For her, this makes sense; she says that people learn *not* to enjoy work when they live in a society in which they have little control over it. Given the chance, she says, they quickly learn to relish making decisions about work, and, at the same moment, to appreciate work itself.

In contrast to Tocqueville's model of democracy, the idea of workplace democracy often begins with an assumption that an "aristocracy of industry" is *inevitable* in a capitalist society. When control of production is in private hands, in a capitalist economy, workers have to sell their labor time. They have no choice; they are just like any other commodity, in this sense, except that, as noted earlier, they cannot just sit in a warehouse for a few years when no one wants to buy them. Goldman would say that if average employees have to hang up their hats as "citizens" when they get to work, then their chances for learning and practicing democracy are too few and far between. Their learning would have to fit into a couple of hours a week after work, and they would know that they were powerless the rest of the week. "After-hours," civic associations might make minor improvements in their lives but they cannot fundamentally change one of the most important and time-consuming relations between people, Goldman says. In contrast, in a workers' collective, democracy becomes a daily practice. Someone might argue that workers would be incompetent to run their own firms, to which Goldman would reply that the bosses' expertise is a sham. Where there are no managers, bosses, or CEOs, but only the employees themselves in control of the big decisions about their work, then the employees *learn how* to make these decisions.

Like Tocqueville, Goldman would say that there is no "self" before society touches it. When a student of mine started an essay by saying, "Society makes us do things we would not otherwise do," this first sentence was already a mistake. Without society, we would not exist, so there is no "otherwise." But Goldman takes another step beyond Tocqueville, by focusing on production. Goldman's approach embodies one of sociology's main premises: we produce the world in which we live, and this world produces us. Just as the essence of a freshwater fish is fresh water, so is our essence *our* shared environment. It is where we live, and without it, we die. But humans, unlike fish, can get together to make complex, reasonable decisions about how to build their shared physical and social environment. If we do not control those decisions, someone else does. If this is so, then our society has a basic problem, because in our society, decisions about production are in private hands, and work is one of the most important places in which we produce our shared world. So when some individuals controls millions more dollars than others, this effectively means that the wealthy have more of a say than the bottom 99 percent, in how to run our society.

The Problem of Bidzina Ivanishvili

Let's take a contemporary example: someone named Bidzina Ivanishvili of the Eastern European republic of Georgia has assets worth over six billion dollars. At the same time, almost 15 percent of Georgians live on less than $1.25 a day (Heritage 2012). Bidzina Ivanishvili wants to run for office. Even if he were a fabulously generous, kindly person, democracy would be hard to imagine in such conditions. How could he realistically lose, when he can buy entire villages? And even if he loses, he could still buy whole villages. As Michael Walzer (1980) argues, democracy cannot hold when one person can indirectly control so much of life.

Take another milder case of privatized decision-making: the case of gardeners in Los Angeles. Goldman would ask, "Who decided that so many people would spend their working hours watering flowers and mowing grass in people's backyards? What if all of their labor went into digging new subway lines, supervising kids after school on the playground, or fixing potholes on the street? Who decides how the society as a whole uses its resources, its creativity, its labor?" Goldman would angrily answer that neither the gardeners themselves nor the public as a whole make the decision. Only those people who have enough money and land for a gardener decide. Instead of a democratic decision-making process, of "one person = one vote," we often have "one dollar = one vote." For Goldman, solutions that do not touch these fundamental relations of production are "band-aid" solutions.

What is worse, for this line of thinking, is that pretending that you are equal citizens is a *harmful* fiction, because if you convince yourself of this, you will not push for real democracy. Real democracy would include more control of the economy than most of us now have. An advocate of workplace democracy would say that these economic decisions should be made democratically, not just with the good of all in *mind*, but *by* the workers themselves.

Because of this, Goldman would not quite approve of Addams' efforts to *ameliorate* conditions within capitalism, because Addams was implicitly acting as if one could realistically have a democracy in a capitalist economy, as if the only question was about how to make it better, within the system. Addams had more faith than Goldman did in the *state*'s ability to regulate the harm that comes from the majority of the population's not having control of the economy. Civic associations could pressure the state in healthful directions, Addams said. Goldman would retort that strengthening the *state* will just create a new kind of power elite, composed of government bureaucrats, as she rightly predicted would happen in the Soviet Union.

So we can see that if we want to line up Goldman along Left–Right lines, it is impossible. The Left usually agrees with Addams in favoring a strong state, to ensure equality of opportunity, and fears corporate power. The Right, in contrast, fears a strong state; is not very worried about inequality; generally favors corporate power; and assumes that corporate heads deserve great power. Some people on the Right think that corporate heads are justified in using their financial power to influence elections; if they were clever enough to get rich running companies, they must also be clever enough to run everything else. Goldman is both extremely Right and extremely Left. She is at the spot where opposites unite: in her passionate quest for equality, she wants to eliminate both the state and the corporations. A slogan from the student uprisings of 1968 could have been taken from Goldman: "Humanity won't be happy till the last bureaucrat is hanged with the guts of the last capitalist." To her mind, when ordinary citizens can cooperatively make decisions all day long about their lives, especially their work lives, but also their lives at schools, and their locales, and in the rest of their daily lives, then neither corporation nor government is necessary. All of life becomes like one big, economically productive, civic association.

Another set of definitions is in order: Goldman's line of thought is usually called "anarcho-socialism," or "anarcho-syndicalism."

The names might set off alarms. Words like "socialist" and "anarchist" have been, in most minds of people in the USA since the 1950s, synonyms for "pure evil." This is a mistake, as people in other countries already know. The horrors inflicted by Stalin and Mao in the name of "socialism" are no more intrinsic to socialism than the horrors of the Inquisition are intrinsic to Christianity. Goldman herself, as noted, predicted the horrors of Stalinism in the Soviet Union. Most Western Europe nations have had socialist governments for some parts of the past century. Most nations in Africa, Asia, and Latin America have had socialist revolutions in the past fifty years. At several points in US history as well, socialist candidates nearly won high positions in government; Upton Sinclair, for example, the author of *The Jungle*, was the California candidate for governor in 1934. He got 37 percent of the vote, while the winner got 48 percent. We have to put our phobias aside momentarily if we want to understand politics in the rest of the globe, and even in our own history.

Many of the ideas from this long and extensive tradition of workplace democracy have been "coopted." Here is another definition: When a radical idea is "coopted," it means that it has been emptied of its original intent and left with only a meaninglessly thin shell of the original idea. When someone like Goldman talks about "worker self-management," she means something very different from the trick that contemporary organizations often pull, of offering employees little "suggestion boxes" and using other little techniques to pretend to put some decisions into employees' hands. High-tech firms often organize workplaces around teamwork, "synergy," sharing ideas to arrive at creative solutions that the employers themselves did not think of (Kunda 1992). This may look like workplace democracy, but as long as the employers have the power to hire and fire employees, or to close up shop and move to another country, it is not what the advocates of workplace democracy mean (Kameo 2010; Kunda 1992). Participation slides into something else that critics call "worker self-exploitation," because, in the fake-ly participatory workplace, if you are clever enough at thinking of a really good labor-saving device that mechanizes the labor you do, you might think yourself out of a job! In a workers' collective, in contrast, if your daydreams led to labor-saving inventions, you do not lose your job. Perhaps you and your fellow employees just work fewer hours, or perhaps you work just as long hours, or perhaps you move onto some new paid daydreaming, making new inventions, sharing with fellow workers in reaping the extra profits that your invention gained for your firm. You keep your job.

The Concept of Eudaimonea and its Relevance for Associations

Despite their differences, Tocqueville, Addams, and Goldman share a great deal. All three focus on the lessons that people learn when they engage in the practical activity of making the world better with fellow citizens. All three describe a step-by-step, pragmatic process of practical problem-solving. All three show that learning the practical arts of democracy works the way learning to play the flute works: no one can learn to play an instrument without habitual, routine, near-daily practice. You play each scale over and over and over until it becomes second-nature. Then, after it has inhabited your body, you can be creative; you can improvise using this scale. After it is as easy as conjugating verbs in your native language is, you can improvise and create something new.

Eudaimonea

The idea that being a good person is easy in a good society, and nearly impossible in a bad one, has been around for a long time. The ancient Greeks' concept of "eudaimonea" summarizes the idea. In a long tradition of social thought, this condition of being in harmony with the forces of good is "eudaimonea" – the prefix "eu" meaning "good," of course, and daimonea being "spirits or gods." Eudaimonea is a kind of moral, spiritual, social happiness that you can attain in a good society, in which being good is in harmony with the rest of society. It may be what the Founding

Fathers meant when they hoped for "life, liberty and the pursuit of happiness." When a new college graduate, to take an example I have witnessed countless times, has to choose between taking an intellectually exciting, creative job with a company that exploits child labor, versus not having a job, versus having a boring job, it is hard for the graduate to be a good person. When he or she must choose between taking an intellectually exciting, creative job with a big polluter, versus not having a job, versus having a boring job, it is hard for the new graduate to reconcile society's demands with his or her own desires to be good according to his or her own standards.

Being able to experience eudaimonea is partly due to "moral luck" (especially as Nussbaum [2001] portrays it)." Eudaimonea would have been relatively inaccessible to a person born in Nazi Germany, or to someone today who does not know that air pollution is a problem. Civic associations, when they work well, make this moral luck less random. Associations can, potentially, inspire people to want to be good, to learn to recognize problems that need fixing, and teach them how to be effective when they try.

When associations work well, they can help create an open-minded inner "self" and a better society, inside and outside, both in one stroke. If, on the other hand, people cannot form self-governing associations, and there is no place for them to learn the arts of self-governance, their inner psyches will, in turn, be more cramped, dry, and fearful, as they are battered by forces which they cannot even imagine controlling. People who live in democracies can, for this line of thought, flower in a way that people who live in non-democracies cannot. This is how Tocqueville, Addams, and Goldman modernize the "eudaimonean" tradition.

Finally, the most fundamental idea on which all three theorists would agree is that self and society mutually create one another. This is sociology's main premise, which all three share. They all ask, therefore, how society can create more of these kinds of selves for whom thoughtful cooperation is second nature. This selfhood, and this society, become second nature – which is, they all say, pretty much the only nature we humans have.

Unfortunately, associations do not always work in the ways that our theorists had hoped. Thoughtless or misplaced volunteering can do serious damage, to volunteers, the recipients of their aid, and to the society at large, for reasons to be dissected in later pages.

2

Volunteering and Political Activism

Both "volunteering" and "political activism" are called "civic engagement," but they are not the same thing. Volunteering and activism blend and separate in many ways. Sometimes, as in Jane Addams' case, volunteering blooms into activism. Sometimes, they are disconnected from one another. As the previous chapter started to show, many practitioners and theorists argue that pretending there is a neutral realm for "volunteering" that can be entirely separate from "politics" is a mistake. This chapter further explores the boundaries of "political activism," showing that there are varied routes to activism, including the one Addams took, which started with innocent-seeming "volunteering."

Usually, though, when we think of volunteering and political activism, we imagine two very different creatures. When I have asked my students to "free associate," by writing down words that come to mind when they think of "volunteer," their words are overwhelmingly warm and friendly: "helpful, caring, fun, selfless, kind-hearted, charity, devote, free, and unity" . . . as well as "looks good on a resume." Words they associated with "activist" are less uniformly positive: "anger, protest, bias, argue, corruption, unhappy, mobs, shouting, hippies, riot," as well as "transform," "awareness," "independence," "freedom," and "challenge." In our shared imagination, the volunteer feels comfortably warm, while the activist either feels too coolly intellectual or too hotheaded. In our collective imagination, the nice, agreeable volunteer reads to pre-schoolers, while the activist pickets and shouts.

43

In reality, the difference is not so stark. In general, yes, volunteers work on fixing problems, in a hands-on, direct way. Yes, activists usually try to change laws, by writing letters to legislators, holding demonstrations and sit-ins – to gain enough power to get a minimum wage established, for example, or workplace safety laws written, environmental protection enforced, bike paths built, faraway political prisoners released, or rainforests preserved. Or activists work more subtly, to transform entrenched customs, even when challenging these entrenched customs evokes great terror in some people – about interracial dating and sexism in the mid twentieth century, or gay marriage today, for example.

However, issues often move from being considered non-politics to politics and vice versa. How does this happen? What difference does it make for a civic association's activities and the meaning of them, if members treat their work as "political" or not?

How Activism Differs from Volunteering

By providing cloth diapers instead of disposable ones, Snugglebumms Diaper Service advertises that it is "changing the world, one diaper at a time." Other companies and nonprofits tell us that we can change the world "one light bulb at a time" (from several companies that sells energy efficient light bulbs), "one smile at a time" (from Operation Smile, an organization that raises funds to help children who are born with a cleft palate and whose parents cannot afford surgery), "one sequin at a time" (Lady Gaga), "one room at a time" (in a book about "green remodeling"), and of course, one person at a time. Usually, volunteers do not routinely question the roots of the problems they aim to solve, but just try to get in there, hands on, directly, to solve the problem, not necessarily caring about its source.

In contrast, political activists

- *Treat the problems that they aim to fix as issues of justice, and of human decision-making, and therefore, as conflicts*, rather than as simply natural, eternal, and inevitable.

- *Expand the domain of political, conscious, democratic decision-making*, moving issues from "private territory" to "public," demanding that people reflect on the issue. Any issue is *potentially* eligible: how we raise our children, teach good manners, define racial categories, reward hard work, use natural resources, produce food, eat, consume, marry, give birth, die – how we survive and how we define thriving.
- *"Connect the dots,"* raise the issue to a level of generality, to see how one issue is connected to another, till the activists have a picture of the whole society.
- *Often operate outside of routine channels*, with civil disobedience or other action that disrupts the taken-for-granted normalcy of the society – sit-ins and boycotts, for example.

(This list summarizes the definition of political activism in Della Porta et al. 2006; also Hamidi 2006.)

Let's treat these elements one at a time.

Treating a Problem as if it is a Result of Human Decision-Making, and Expanding the Realm of Politics

When civic associations make it clear that a problem is not natural and inevitable, but has a human solution, their first step has to be to name the problem. Some examples from the mid twentieth century of newly named problems include "urban blight," "silent spring (for a spring that had so much pollution, many birds didn't sing, but died instead)" "child abuse," and "the problem that has no name" (what early feminist Betty Friedan called the vague unease that housewives felt). In the 1970s and 1980s came "marital rape," and "environmental racism." "Marital rape" was invented because, before the 1980s, in most states, a husband could force his wife to have sex against her will and it was not considered "rape," but just unpleasant. Environmental racism refers to our society's disproportionate frequency of locating toxic dumps and industries in disadvantaged, minority neighborhoods

(Bullard 2000). Naming a problem, in turn, allows for further action on it.

When the phrase "environmental racism" arose in the 1980s, the phrase itself unified problems that had previously been seen as separate: the toxic dump in an African-American neighborhood, the uranium storage unit next door to the Native-American reservation, and the chemical refinery in the Latino neighborhood. With the new name, they all become "see-able" as cases of the newly named category. Naming a problem is crucial, then. Once people name a problem as "politics," and not just natural and inevitable, they can "see" many things that once seemed separate as fitting into this new category.

The most spectacular examples of the past three decades involve issues surrounding gender, family, sexuality, and mental health. There was no name for "child abuse" or "neglect" before the middle of the twentieth century! Plenty of children underwent what we would *now* call abuse or neglect before that, but there was no law forbidding it, and no legal definition of it (Nelson 1986). There was no phrase "child abuse" in colloquial speech. It was just considered an unfortunate occurrence. This made it hard for people to see a wide range of acts as "cases of" child abuse: one child had sex with a grandparent, another was locked in a closet, another was beaten, but these problems were not seen as related, not "on the same table" (Foucault 1989). Sometimes, the new category is a result of professionals, such as mental-health clinicians, becoming activists of sorts, as in the case of "child abuse" or "post-traumatic stress disorder." However the new category originated, it allows people to "see" separate items as sharing a key characteristic, and simultaneously, they can start to talk about it. They can discover other people who share the problem, and they can do something together about this newly named category. In the process of talking about it, they can start to see if it is a problem that is inevitable and natural – not amenable to a political solution – or if there might be an issue of justice and politics involved.

Of course, naming a social problem is not like naming a cat. Whatever one names one's cat is its name. In contrast, not everyone will agree that "environmental racism" exists, even after someone has invented the name. With marital rape, for example, there is an argument, not over whether husbands sometimes force wives to have sex at gunpoint or knifepoint during marriage, but whether it is a logical possibility for that activity to be "rape" in the first place. A Right-wing icon and activist, Phyllis Schlafly, disputed the logical possibility of marital rape, saying, "By getting married, the woman has consented to sex, and I don't think you can call it rape." This was part of a speech she gave in 2007, not in prehistoric times, for her hosts, the Bates College Republicans (Leonard 2007). Legislators over the years have used the same reasoning to deny the logical possibility of rape in marriage. When activists try to name a problem, other activists and policy-makers will disagree that such a thing exists, only certain names will stick, and not just any name will suffice. Some will argue over the data, saying that a particular man did not rape his wife in a particular case, while others will take it to a political level, arguing over the conceptual possibility of the category's existence at all.

Over the past few decades, civic associations have started to address many problems that once seemed purely personal and private. The definitions of politics keep expanding. Consider this list that Robert Dahl, a preeminent mid-century political scientist, composed, in 1961, of topics that were obviously *not* politics: "food, sex, love, family, work, play, shelter, comfort, friendship, social esteem, and the like" (cited in Schudson 1997: 240). All of these topics have come under political scrutiny since Dahl's time. We could add to this list of formerly un-political topics: Art becomes a political question when there are revivals of ethnic styles, battles over sexual images in museums, or arguments over what to count as "art" versus what to count as "folkloric crafts" (and therefore, not worth millions of dollars and not worth archiving in museums). Birth and death become political questions when people argue about natural childbirth, or assisted suicide. Ethnic and religious identity becomes a political question when people argue about bilingual education or headscarves. Medicine becomes politics when people argue about AIDS research, health care funding, and genetic testing. This is just a very shortened list of some obvious candidates for topics that have gone from "not-politics" to "politics" since Dahl's time. How do people decide to treat some shared problems as worthy of political solutions? It is *not* that some problems are *intrinsically* political and others are not. It is almost impossible to think of a personal, or local problem that is just completely unconnected to the broader society. Almost everything is *potentially* "politics."

Take the problem of physical or developmental disability. Disability was once considered a simply natural, biological problem. Before 1975, if you or your child had a disability, it was just your problem. If you could not enter the public school's door in your wheelchair, or could not stay in the public school because you had a learning disability, the school sent you home or sent you to a school that threw all disabled people together, no matter what their particular disability was. Usually, it was then your parents' (usually mother's) responsibility to provide you with an education that matched your abilities.

A great transformation started with little civic associations of disabled people and their relatives, organized initially for mutual aid in the form of emotional support, care-giving exchange, and information exchange. By the 1960s, partly taking their inspiration from the Civil Rights Movement, some people were trying to make disability into a political issue (Pettinicchio 2011). Disability goes from being a problem that seems natural and inevitable to one that we, the people, have a duty to ameliorate. The Individuals with Disabilities Education Act of 1973 is a culmination of years of quiet pressure. It states that all children have a *right* to an education. The right expanded to include access to any buildings that receive state funding, such as courts, medical offices that use public money (such as Medicare), public libraries, public pools, and more. So, we now have sidewalk ramps for wheelchairs, "kneeling busses" that have a ramp that unfolds from the bus to the sidewalk, so that people in wheelchairs, old people and anyone else who can't climb stairs can still enter the bus, and more. We as a society have decided to pay for this, and when people are on the bus and the driver lowers the ramp for a person in a wheelchair, the other passengers almost all, almost always, politely wait. We pay, and we wait, because we have decided, implicitly, that a good society is one in which people do not just leave the disabled to suffer on their own, or to rely on the kindness of relatives (Kittay 2000).

Step-by-step, these associations had "politicized" the issue, in small ways at first, until finally, it reached the level of a change in the nation's laws. In the grander scheme of human history, this was a massive and incredibly rapid transformation. Before the 1960s, disability was considered a misfortune, an act of God or nature. The wheel of fate had turned and you were on the bottom. After the 1960s, people started treating the issue as one of rights, not just fate; as injustice, not just bad luck; as a problem that people can and should fix rather than leave up to God or nature (Pitkin 1980). Here, as in Tocqueville's model, people joined in civic action with the aim of swaying "moral luck," by forcing a change in *conditions*. It is hard to be an equal member of society if you are at the bottom and cannot go to school, or the library, or mount city hall's steps. It is also, perhaps surprisingly, equally hard to be a fair-minded person if you are at the top, and cannot hear the ideas of the people who sit excluded at the bottom of the staircase. Whether at the top or bottom, making access easier makes eudaimonea easier for everyone to experience.

The example of disability rights shows a way that activities that start off as "natural" comes to be seen as "subject to human decision-making," and how something that starts off as "non-political" comes to be seen as "political." It became clear to the disability rights advocates that just carrying each disabled person up the steps, one at a time, was too hard, and humiliating to the person who was being carried. The problem was the conditions, not the individual. The advocates became political activists.

Connecting the Dots

"Connecting the dots" is a shorthand way of talking about the second element that distinguishes activism from typical volunteer work. Fixing a problem like marital rape, or legal segregation, or pollution might seem far removed from the overarching, radical changes that something like Goldman's image of workers' self-management suggests. But history shows that once people start challenging one simple-seeming law or custom – start to pull just one thread out of the social fabric – the whole cloth seems to unravel for them, like a knitted scarf that started the day with only one loose piece of yarn and ends the day completely undone.

A good illustration of this unraveling process comes from the stories of the American college students who went to the South in the 1960s to register black people to vote. The lives of these students resembled Jane Addams' in many ways: mainly from upper-middle class backgrounds, these hopeful youth wanted to do something useful for society. When they first signed up, most of them assumed that the problem would be relatively easy to solve: just ride on down to the South and sign up more black voters. When these Freedom Riders, as they were called, got there, they discovered the local police were white and were usually on the side of the racists, either through personal conviction, political ties, blood ties, or all three. The higher-up, non-local legislators in the South were no help, either. Powerful Southerners often worked hand-in-hand with powerful Northerners, too. Like Addams, these hopeful students realized that if they wanted to fix the problem, they would have to change much more than the voter registration process (all of this is recounted in McAdam 1990). Jane Addams started with helping families one at a time, and ending up pressing for new laws about child labor; the Northern college students were similarly starting to see the whole scarf unravel.

Non-routine action and playful politics

Often, though not always, political activism differs from volunteering in a third way: by working outside the normal channels for registering complaints – not by sending petitions and letters to legislators, but by more direct means. Protestors from Gandhi to Martin Luther King to contemporary Occupy activists have often *started* by trying to work within the normal rules, but then have concluded that working within the rules does not always work.

When Civil Rights Movement activists began to stage sit-ins at segregated lunch counters, and to sit at the front of the bus in segregated busses, they knew they would get arrested, but saw this "civil disobedience" as a step toward the greater good. Writing from a Birmingham jail, Martin Luther King said,

> We know through painful experience that freedom is never voluntarily given by the oppressor; it must be demanded by the oppressed. Frankly, I have yet to engage in a direct action campaign that was "well timed" in the view of those who have not suffered unduly from the disease of segregation. For years now I have heard the word "Wait!" It rings in the ear of every Negro with piercing familiarity. This "Wait" has almost always meant "Never." (King 1963)

It might seem as if civil disobedience is mainly aimed at simply getting the lunch, resting the tired feet on the bus, making the injustice go away. But more importantly, activists commit civil disobedience to draw attention to their cause. Activists notice that if no one gets beaten up, their demonstrations do not make it into the news (Della Porta et al. 2006). So, they stage pickets, demonstrations, and commit acts of civil disobedience, in hopes of getting media attention.

In the past twenty years, however, pickets, demonstrations, and even civil disobedience have become routine. While there still are, rarely, some completely spontaneous, unplanned political events, and some activists who smash windows and light bonfires, most activists plan most political events in advance. To stage a demonstration, protesters usually get a "parade permit" from the police. When the activists plan on going further, to conduct civil disobedience, there are usually no surprises there, either: Protesters usually tell the police precisely what they are planning, so that they can get arrested without becoming permanently disabled by out-of-control, panicked police. The protesters go through a "training" in how to commit civil disobedience without becoming injured. For example, they learn to hold their hands apart and not to make abrupt gestures so as not to appear threatening to police and so as not to be seen as "resisting arrest;" they learn not to wear contact lenses in case the police use tear gas; to make sure they have a buddy who will know their whereabouts when they get arrested; to turn to the side and relax if police charge toward them; not to have weapons or drugs on them; and more.

This *routinely* non-routine action makes for an interesting relationship between protesters and police. While the police normally defend the status quo against the protesters, they also sometimes have to defend the protesters against counter-protesters. This happened, for example, when anti-immigration activists came to harass the large immigrant rights marches of 2007. It happens when the Los Angeles police follow Critical Mass bike rides as the hundreds of bike riders take over entire streets so that cars cannot pass. The police are supposed to keep the bikes in order but also to protect the bike riders from the cars.

Sometimes, protesters try to convince the police to switch sides. Anti-nuclear war activists in the 1980s held workshops on how to talk to the police in a persuasive, non-antagonistic way, with the aim of showing them that the police themselves stood to lose from nuclear build-up, too. Later, Occupy activists tried to convince police in many locales that the police were part of the "99 percent," too. Sometimes, this strategy worked spectacularly well. In Albany, NY, for example, the police defied the government, by publically announcing that they would refuse to arrest Occupy protesters unless they were seriously damaging state property (Rudolf 2012). And over the course of history, change has sometimes, indeed, included the police and armed forces' switching sides, going from defending the government to joining the protesters against the government in power.

When formerly "non-routine" actions like sitting in and boycotting become routine, some activists go further afield, looking for new ways to break routine so they can bring attention to their cause. The gay rights group Act Up, for example, staged "kiss-ins" at ice-cream parlors in the 1980s. Another example of activists' creative quest to find non-routine ways to get their message out comes from arguments over how to teach evolution in public schools. The Kansas City School Board voted to force teachers to teach evolution as if it were just a theory, alongside the Bible's theory of Creation, in biology classes. In protest, the Church of the Flying Spaghetti Monster formed, to press the School Board to make sure that all pupils *also* learn about *their* religion's views of creation. Is the Flying Spaghetti Monster part of a religion deserving the same respect the creationists' story gets? The church of the Flying Spaghetti Monster's website says it is, arguing that, "Most of us do not believe (that) a religion . . . requires literal belief in order to provide spiritual enlightenment . . . many in other religions don't literally believe their scripture . . . (3/3/2012, from http://www.venganza.org/about/)"

And all of this stands in contrast to the main comparison group for this chapter: volunteers, who never have to worry about Flying Spaghetti Monsters, or the effect of tear gas on contact lenses.

Puzzles for Activist and Volunteer Groups

For all of their differences, activists and volunteers face some similar puzzles.

Expanding the scope of decision-making, the first element of activism, comes with potential problems. When activism starts to turn routine habits and customs – be they smoking, flirting with one's colleague, or raping one's wife – into public, political decisions, it can be hard to know where to stop, and it can lead to a trampling of privacy.

As Tocqueville argued, democracies allow the people as a whole to decide where to place the line dividing private life from public life. In democracies, Tocqueville argued, people use public powers to ensure and protect privacy. Contemporary examples include making sure that you are allowed to practice whatever religion you want and are not thrown out of school for speaking your mind. These seem utterly reasonable, but politicizing seemingly private decisions could go too far. Many utopian novels of the late 1800s to early 1900s envisioned a society that unified work, family, and everything else into a monstrosity that the authors imagined would be a total political solution to everything! In Charlotte Perkins Gilman's late nineteenth-century science fiction utopia, *Herland*, for example, the whole collective raised babies, so babies would not become attached just to one or two parents, and so that parents would not selfishly care more about their own child than any other. This kind of arrangement is not impossible: a similar family system worked in Samoa for thousands of years before the Europeans came (Mead 1971 [1928]), and the socialist kibbutzim in twentieth-century Israel had such a structure, as well. However, when squatters (people who take over empty, boarded-up apartments, and don't pay rent) in Geneva share cooking, cleaning, and all of their living space, it can feel too intrusive and overwhelming – "unbearable" (Breviglieri 1999). While such arrangements for living, working, and childraising are certainly possible, a civic organization may well ask whether they are desirable.

The question that people in civic associations can decide, that is, is how to draw the line between public and private. Answering it is more complicated than it seems. In the most contemporary societies, we think we treat love and sex as "private," but we make many fine exceptions: between teacher and student; between doctor and patient; between family members; between humans and sheep; between people under eighteen years old and people over eighteen; between races until 1967 in some states in the USA (many states had laws against interracial marriage till then); between people of the same sex. In all of those cases, we think of ourselves as treating love as a private affair that activists are "politicizing," but in fact, our society already does politicize sex, love, and family, making them into public, legal questions that laws already judge. It might seem tempting to say that all such decisions should be private, till a child dies of abuse or neglect. Seemingly intrusive public regulation seems less intrusive after a disaster. Usually, ordinary people do not discuss this fine line-drawing very clearly, but theorists argue that they should. The job should, according to some theorists, be one for civic associations to decide (Habermas 1985)

Drawing the boundary is even more puzzling in a multicultural society than it might be in a more homogenous one. How do we decide, for example, what to count as abuse, when different cultures disagree? In France, part of the argument against wearing a burka – the long robe, hood, and face covering that certain

Muslims demand for women – is a form of abuse, preventing women from enjoying full-body movement and access to sunlight. But forbidding it in schools and public meetings seems like a violation of the society's vision of religion as one's own private business, not publicly regulated.

Another dilemma with "expanding the scope of decision-making" is that it would probably be impossible for workers to hold a public, thoughtful discussion about all aspects of production, about the cost of bamboo versus wood, molybdenum versus titanium, for example. For this, it seems to make sense to use the market, and money, as a way of making decisions; the market could be an efficient mechanism for assigning value that did not require a long discussion. We will come back to this in later chapters, especially where we discuss Corporate Social Responsibility.

Problems with "connecting the dots"

When activists start to see how pulling out one stitch might set the whole scarf unraveling, this can also pose dilemmas. It is hard to sustain the life-changing commitment of people like the Freedom Riders. They went South and came back unable to fit into their former lives. The transformation was painful at the moment, and even twenty years later, their divorce rates were still higher and incomes lower than their counterparts who had wanted to but, through happenstance, not been able to go on the trip South in the 1960s (McAdam 1990). This kind of painful transformation makes little, once-a-week, "pick up litter in the park" type volunteering look appetizingly harmless. It makes activism look potentially too difficult and risky for ordinary people. And perhaps it is better to have a lot of people who are a little committed to their social missions than to have only a few people who are a lot committed. The "strength of weak ties" can be as strong as the thousands of thin cables that hold up the Golden Gate Bridge.

Another risk that comes with seeing the big picture is that people might get discouraged when they see how the little problem they aim to fix is connected to big problems. They might feel powerless and just go home. For example, participants in volunteer groups often shy away from talking about anything beyond the very "do-able" tasks at hand. In *Avoiding Politics* (Eliasoph 1998), we encounter parent volunteers who know about the political roots of local problems that affect their children, such as the lack of state funds for repairing the school building, even when the library ceiling caves in, or the race riots at the school, or the 30–acre toxic pit at a military base a mile away. They know about the political connections. While raising funds for their children's high school, for example, parents in a typical parent association conducted a long discussion about how to sell steamed hot dogs at track meets. One member said,

> I looked all over for a machine that can roast hot dogs continuously so we don't get a backlog when all the kids come up to the stand at once. So, I found one at this restaurant supplier. They're offering us a discount, so we should write them a thank you note. It's called a Royal Dog Steamer, and it can steam foot longs, Polish dogs, hot links, regular dogs, sausages, you name it, about twenty at a time! (Eliasoph 1998)

Outside of meetings, behind the scenes, "backstage," participants talk about these "bigger" issues. These volunteers are not doing what Tocqueville would have predicted; they are not learning how to connect their seemingly personal affairs with big political issues. To keep having faith in their own volunteer efforts, they need to uphold a can-do spirit. In their minds, this means not talking about discouraging problems that they can't immediately fix. *They assume that it would be too discouraging to talk about politics, even while they are steaming the hot dogs.*

In theory, if we think of Addams, we imagine that grassroots volunteering and politics are on a continuum, bleeding into one another. Here, paradoxically, volunteering makes political action more difficult. These volunteers were worried that their fragile can-do spirit would collapse if they talked about the bigger issues surrounding their kids' high school. Talking about bigger issues would be "inappropriate" and "out of place" in their civic associations.

Working outside of routine channels also poses puzzles for civic associations, beyond the obvious problem of being risky. The dramatic methods that activists used to call attention to an issue might drive the public away from it. The sit-in, the outdoors encampment, the mass arrest in the capitol building: all of this can start to take attention away from the movement's goals. It becomes especially difficult to keep the movement's "eyes on the prize," because if police attack protesters, the protesters then devote their time to seeking medical and legal aid, instead of publicizing the issues they had originally aimed to publicize. Several short newspaper reports in November and December 2011 in the *Los Angeles Times*, for example, reported that police beat protesters at Occupy Oakland, without once mentioning why Occupy Oakland existed.

Efforts to Separate Volunteers from Politics

However hard it is to connect volunteering to politics, disconnecting them might be more risky. One political scientist has gained international acclaim by arguing that civic associations "make democracy work" even when they are completely disconnected from politics. Any kind of togetherness works to build democracy, Robert Putnam (2000) says, even the kind that develops in informal associations like bowling leagues and singing groups. His evidence is that the mid twentieth century was both the high point of civic engagement and the high point for political engagement, as indicated by high voting rates, numbers of times people contacted politicians, and other measures. This is a false correlation in numerous ways.

Critics of Putnam say that his work has gotten wide play because he offers a nice feel-good argument, which suffers not only from the flaw of being incorrect (Skocpol 2003), but also for leading to destructive policies that value "volunteering" at the expense of "politics." First of all, Putnam counted many political activist groups (such as the Sierra Club) as "civic" associations that he said caused "political" engagement, so he was saying, in effect, that political activism caused political activism (Sobieraj and White 2004; Skocpol 2003). Furthermore, the years he points to as the high water mark for American civic life were also the years in which the gap between rich and poor was at an all-time low, and he did not fully grasp the connection between the two trends, according to critics. This trend was partly the federal government's response to many civic associations' fight for policies to promote equality. The equality for which the civic associations fought promoted, in turn, more civic engagement; in a society that has a relatively small gap between rich and poor, civic associations thrive. Putnam's critics argue, for example, that the state lessened inequality when it responded to civic associations' demands for health benefits for veterans, or for Social Security, for example, in the late 1800s and early 1900s. These programs benefited all veterans and all old people (Skocpol 2003: 71), not just those who fell below some poverty line. Associations helped enforce the policies that led to relative class equality which, in turn, allowed strong associations to grow and thrive. In these ways, a strong state with strong welfare programs did not crowd out civic life, despite some Right-wing pundits' claims to the contrary. To the contrary, a strong state that promoted a somewhat egalitarian society went *with* a strong civic life that was embroiled with the political affairs of the day. Another place to see this mutual embroilment is in the local chapters' internal affairs. Women in the Henry, Nebraska chapter of a statewide association gathered in 1916 to discuss "South Dakota Laws of Interest to Women and Children," "Our National Defenses Today," and "Immigration," for example (Skocpol 2003: 122). So, rather than imagining a wall between civic associations and the state, we should imagine a cycle between the two.

Putnam's critics also demonstrate that the civic associations that pressed for these egalitarian policy changes were big, powerful, national associations, not little, local groups. These national federations were organized into locals, the way the Boy Scouts is. These were the associations whose placards used to be attached to the sign announcing a city limits like the Lions Club, Rotary, Elks, and Moose. Big civic clubs were scorned by intellectuals of the era, in novels such as Sinclair Lewis' popular mid-century novels *Babbitt, Main Street,* and *Arrowsmith,* which depicted them as gathering places for dull, smug, drunk businessmen. They may have been that, but part of what made those associations popular was also the excitement of feeling that one was "part of something bigger." It was not little local bowling leagues and singing groups that made democracy work, but the nationally "federated" associations whose members saw themselves as important political actors that did. We will come back to this question of whether state and civic associations work in see-saw relation to one another in chapter 3.

It's Not Always an "Either-Or" Between "Volunteer" and "Politics"

Volunteers often want the hands-on task of helping someone directly, but volunteering sometimes becomes more convincing, and therefore, more inspiring when it is connected to politics. When you are helping the one child learn math, it is hard to ignore the thirty-four others in the room who are not getting any one-on-one help. You might start to wonder if hiring a few more staff people in the school would be effective. You might feel stupid volunteering to spend hundreds of hours helping one homeless person instead of spending that same amount of time trying to get the government or a corporation to fund housing for a thousand homeless people. But then, you might realize that to get more staff at the school or to get housing for thousands of homeless people, you would have to organize an activist group, and so, if you are a typical American volunteer, your mind might shut off at that moment that the possibility arose in your head. You might end up feeling powerless.

Political activism, on the other hand, also has its limitations. Activism lets people see the big picture, but it can feel abstract and dry. The results are long term and mediated, not yet tangible. Sometimes, it seems to be all about writing letters, signing petitions, making convincing arguments and staging public events. Activism can sometimes become more emotionally real to people when it is connected to volunteering. Sometimes, a person can learn something from directly helping someone, even if it is something that the volunteer cannot later put into words (Bender 2003). Sometimes, people cannot get this feeling by writing, picketing, or reading – except maybe by reading novels and poetry. Ideally, one would want both: to unify "caring about" an issue with "taking care of" someone or something (Tronto 1994).

Take the problem of traffic congestion in cities like Los Angeles, Madrid, Bogotá, Paris, and Mexico City. People want to fix the problem right away by taking over the streets with masses of bikes. They want a tangible experience of traveling in different conditions right away. They also want to change policies, so that the experience will be easier to have in the future. These cities are not known for their peaceful, green streets; riding a bike in them is a death-defying feat at the moment. Bike activists have extracted promises from many cities to construct networks of bike paths, allowing people to commute on their own steam instead of fossil fuels. This is an important policy change for which political activists can advocate, but if nothing changed but the pavement and the regulations, it would not be enough. Bicycle activists in these and dozens of other cities around the world have been taking over streets for a day at a time, colonizing space that is usually filled with cars and trucks, and using it for bikes, skateboards, roller skates, anything but gas-powered vehicles. All of these are aimed at showing people that the streets can become recreational spaces for pleasant exercise, fresh air, and sociability. The activists, that is, have to lure people into *wanting to* ride bikes on city streets. Activists in different societies balance the private versus the public justifications for their activism, as an ongoing study of bike activism worldwide shows (Luhtakallio, Carrel, and Eliasoph 2011).

The original event that took over the city streets for a day was in Bogotá. Its original aim was to reduce crime by getting people out on the street and acquainted with neighbors. Now, activists all over have copied it, but as it travels the world, it takes different forms. In Los Angeles, they marvel over the streets' quietness when the cars are gone; in Helsinki, they take pride in fighting global climate change while slogging through the rain; in Paris, they mount their "vélos" (the word for bike in French) fiercely claiming to be starting a "vélorution;" and meanwhile, in Madrid, there is "ciclonudista!"

If people just focused on attaining their policy goals, they would miss the process. When people connect the means and the ends, they learn new things along the way. The process opens up new feelings, thoughts, actions, and discoveries. In the process of volunteering to enact the change that they hope to institutionalize, people discover pleasures and horrors that they had not anticipated – the quiet sound of a city street without cars, a view of a trash problem that no one had publicized, the wind in their hair, a chance encounter that becomes a budding romance, a vision of childhood in slums with no green places for play. None of this would have happened if they had passed each scene in a car. In Los Angeles, they discover that it is faster to bike from point A to B when there is no car traffic than it is to drive the same distance in the usual amount of car traffic. This is a discovery with *major implications* for urban design. As we saw in Jane Addams' work, hands-on, non-conflictual, volunteer-style engagement yields valuable insights for policy-makers.

A similar mix of hands-on and abstract involvement surrounds questions about food. Problems related to food include poor nutrition even in wealthy countries, rising obesity rates, a loss of knowledge of customary farming techniques and the environmental destruction that goes with that, as well as a simple lack of food. A gratifyingly hands-on, volunteer-style way of addressing all of these is to start community gardens. It is educational to watch the food grow, people come together socially, and the result tastes better than the grocery store equivalent. When a community garden works, it is a tangible experience that leads to discoveries about the local society that participants could not have guessed by just reading about the neighborhood. But it is not enough, because at best, they do not raise enough food for more than a few dinners for a few families. So, beyond starting community gardens, neighborhoods can lure farmers' markets into the area. But that is not enough, either, since many people never learned how to cook fresh vegetables. So, beyond this, volunteers can teach people about cooking, as in a program run by volunteers called Quick! Help for Meals, at farmers' markets in Los Angeles. Beyond these local, hands-on, volunteer-style solutions, are more "political" solutions: the Los Angeles City Council took a vote a few years ago that limited the numbers of fast-food chains per block in neighborhoods that have no normal grocery stores. The hope was that grocery stores would move to these impoverished neighborhoods, and indeed, some have done so. Beyond *this* is national policy action, such as one organization's agenda of pressing Congress to cut the billions of dollars of subsidies that go to agri-business companies. One NGO, the California Public Interest Research Group explains the connection by saying that Twinkies are cheap while carrots are expensive, not because carrots are harder to make. Rather, it is that billions of dollars in the past decade have gone to subsidize agribusinesses that use the subsidies to grow crops that they convert into unhealthful food additives that are more profitable for them to sell, such as high fructose corn syrup (http://calpirg.org/issues/cap/stop-subsidizing-obesity-0).

Ideally, organizations can join the volunteer and activists' approaches, but this is not always possible. For some issues, volunteering is not an option. For example, people who want to help political prisoners can join Amnesty International groups to write protest letters to the governments that are holding the prisoners. Amnesty International also holds events to teach people about this distant suffering. There is not much that a person can do, hands-on, to help a person who is in solitary confinement, even if the prison is nearby, much less across the world. So local Amnesty International chapters have ways of making the experience feel real to participants. They read novels and memoirs, for example, or become semi-expert in the region on which their group focuses (Gray 2012).

More often, the volunteer approaches and the activist approaches can go hand-in-hand. Activism has to make the nutritious food or the bike riding possible, through policies that create bike lanes, and that make healthful food accessible to all people, not just wealthy ones. But it also has to work on convincing people of the spirit of the law, not just the letter: they have to *want* to exercise, and to *enjoy* healthful food. Here, as Addams would insist, there will always be puzzles. One puzzle is that when people come into a neighborhood and tell the local people that their eating and exercise habits are all wrong, it might seem paternalistic and condescending. This is Addams' point about asking to become perplexed; democratic inquiry doesn't have an end; there is no final solution. Democracy is an experiment, but unlike experiments on chemicals, the objects of the democratic experiment (humans) are also sometimes designing the experiment, or designing experiments of their own. The experiment changes the people, who then can design new experiments based on their new selves in their new society. It's an endless spiral of change and inquiry that produces more change that produces more inquiry.

Eating, housing, transportation, clothing: for all these activities and many more, it is important not to take it for granted that an issue is naturally "political" or not. Rather, an observer who wants to understand what makes any particular civic group tick can ask him or herself, "*How* do people in a civic association connect or disconnect 'caring about people' and 'caring about politics?'"

3

Civic Association, the Market, and Government: How Do Different Societies Balance Them Differently?

"Common sense" tells us to expect the state, the market, and civic life to do different things. Governments build public goods like schools, highways, and armies. Market organizations sell things at a profit. Civic volunteers do nice things for free.

However, once again, common sense is too simplistic. Activities move in and out of the spheres of market, government, and civic association over time. For example, for most of the past century, elementary education has been the government's job, not that of voluntary civic associations. But nowadays, some people want parent volunteers to help run charter schools. Some others want profit-making firms to sponsor elementary education, with fee-based education and current events programs that have ads in them. Education is coming up for sale, in a way that was unthinkable a few decades ago, not to mention a few centuries ago, when most elementary education happened in religious institutions. The walls separating civic associations, market, and state, as well as family and religion, might seem solid, but they are not.

Civic associations occupy different social spaces in different nations. In France, they were outlawed till 1901. For an American, it would be inconceivable that a democracy such as France could outlaw civic associations. Almost by definition, a society that outlawed associations would not, by Americans' definition, be a democracy. In Nordic nations, in contrast, the government has financed civic associations. This, too, would baffle most Americans, for whom common sense says that civic associations that are not separate from the state are not independent or authentic enough to qualify as real civic associations.

Different nations draw the balance between state, market, and civic life differently, creating different "eco-systems" in which civic associations can grow well or poorly (Edwards 2009). This chapter first asks: What place do civic associations hold in American society? In other societies? What are healthy ways of balancing between the state, market, and civic arena? If they go too far out of balance, does democracy collapse?

Is There a Trade-Off Between a Lively Civic Life and Strong Welfare State?

If the State Withdraws, Do Civic Associations and the Market Step In to Fix Social Ills?

Some scholars, pundits and politicians say that little, local associations are the keystones of democracy, and they see them as *an alternative* to the state and politics. They say that associations work best when they are informal, purely local, disconnected from the government, and apolitical. The first President Bush's image of "a thousand points of light" was a beautiful metaphor for this image of civic engagement, showing many unconnected idealists spread across the wide, black sky, each separately preserving the galaxy of democracy. In the same years, Prime Minister Margaret Thatcher offered a similar idea in a speech to the Women's Royal Voluntary Service in 1981: "The willingness of men and women to give service is one of freedom's greatest safeguards. It ensures that caring remains *free from political control*" (Wheeler 2005; my italics).

Both leaders imagined state and civic associations as being on a see-saw: more of one leads to less of the other, and the best thing government can do is stay away from civic associations, to allow them to work freely, so that "caring remains free from political control." As one US nonprofit executive put it in the 1970s, government funding "contaminates" volunteering (quoted in Smith and Lipsky 1995).

These scholars and politicians assume that if the government stops providing help, volunteers will take up the slack, to meet the needs of preschoolers, sick people, old people, students, disabled people, the environment, and the rest. They assume that enlisting voluntary associations to solve social problems is *morally better* than having the state solve them. They assume that associations are uncontaminated and pure only when untouched by state funds. And they assume that care given by families, neighbors, and friends is of a *better quality* than paid care, because they assume unpaid care-giving is about love, not money. They say it is *better for the whole society*, because it builds informal, flexible but loyal bonds in a way that laws and policies could never accomplish. While the image is magnetically appealing, there are good reasons to doubt that it is usually accurate. Often, people need more long-term, steady, professional help, or more material help such as food and housing, than after-hours volunteers can supply.

In political debates, nevertheless, when politicians extol the virtues of *civic* life and the *market*, while scorning the *state*, they often assume that more "state" always means less "civic," while at the same time, for this view, "civic" and "market" go together. People who adhere to this view want to balance the tripod by putting as little weight as possible on the state. For the reasoning behind their idea that "civic" and "market" are harmonious, while "civic" and "state" are on a see-saw opposite each other, we can return to Putnam. He says that little local voluntary associations are not only good for democracy but also good for the economy. Like Bush and Thatcher, Putnam says that coming together in informal civic groups builds trust and social networks. This, in turn, greases the wheels of the economy, because when people develop informal friendly companionship in associations, sellers and buyers can find each other quickly and painlessly, through the pleasures of social networks, this theory says. The mutual trust that comes from shared civic engagement lets sellers trust buyers to pay them, even if the sellers do not send the police or a collection agency, and it lets buyers trust that they will get what they paid for. This trust is harder to attain and more necessary nowadays, for two reasons. First, we trade with total strangers across the globe. Second, we are past the era of selling easily recognizable objects like goats and chickens, but in an era in which our most lucrative objects of trade are objects whose quality is hard to verify at a glance, such as chemical liquids and mineral powders, apps and chips.

For this image of civic associations that balances the moral tripod toward civic and market and away from state solutions, state regulation of the economy becomes, at best, icing on the cake of a pre-existing moral order that is constantly replenished by civic associations. For this view, the state cannot create moral order, but only reinforce the moral order that civic associations create. Not only does state regulation of the market become superfluous icing on the cake, but it can easily become a hindrance, because, in this worldview, people who have a warm feeling of community will regulate themselves in a more natural, flexible way than any laws could ever accomplish. People who are freely engaged in the market and in free associations will have good attitudes and will barely need the state, according to this perspective.

When we emphasize the good attitudes that people learn in civic associations, and de-emphasize the state, we get arguments like the ones we have heard regarding the banking crisis. Many pundits focused exclusively on "the culture" and "attitudes" on Wall Street, rather than also focusing on the fact that the state had steadily stripped away one regulation of the financial industry after another over the course of the previous three decades.

In the USA and the UK, especially, "privatization" and "deregulation" have become buzzwords for people who do not trust experts and government planners. The word "deregulation" means that government stops constraining businesses, so that the regulations for which Jane Addams fought – for workplace safety or a minimum wage, for example – are weakened, or no longer in effect. Again, the article of faith here is that people will regulate themselves, through unpaid, voluntary civic associations. The word "privatization" means that formerly state-run enterprises or spaces – parks, schools, or beaches, for example – are converted into for-profit businesses or NGOs. Instead of everyone's pooling their tax money to keep beaches clean, whether they personally go to the beach or not, they pay only if they go. And they go only if they can afford it. If you cannot afford it or if there are not enough fee-paying clients, the private company should convert the enterprise into something more profitable, in the "privatization" model – turn a beach into an oil-drilling area, or a mountain campgrounds into a logging business. If you are a child whose parents cannot afford to pay for the "privatized" swimming pool, you do not learn to swim. If your parents cannot afford books, and the libraries start charging for services on a fee-per-use basis, too bad, unless a charity steps in.

Such policies are based on the assumption that less government will mean both more vibrant associations and a better economy. Civic associations are an essential element in this picture: markets by themselves would be too brutal, but, according to the theory, a charity will step in, because once the state steps *out*, people's freely charitable and caring feeling will blossom: The child *will* learn to swim and *will* have access to books; the homeless people *will* get a soup kitchen, and the process of helping the less fortunate will make the volunteers into the kinds of good citizens whom Tocqueville imagined. Aiding the poor is supposed to build the volunteers' character. This, paradoxically, makes poverty necessary for social well-being, in a sense, as the society needs poor people for their virtue-producing effect on volunteers (Poppendieck 1999).

The view that civic associations indirectly build the economy is inspiring. The view that volunteers inevitably will step in to bring the child the books and the homeless person the soup when the state stops providing the libraries, homes, and food is also inspiring. However, the contemporary evidence for both parts of the argument is highly disputed.

Some evidence for the first image comes from Robert Putnam's historical study that compares northern and southern Italy since the Renaissance. In this case, the theory does fit very well. The problem is that politicians use the idea even in cases where it does not fit. In this study, we learn that northern Italy had a dense network of free associations, such as choral groups and theater clubs, while southern Italy had hardly any free associations, but many coerced, involuntary memberships in the church and family based associations like the Mafia. The North has been more afflu-ent than the South for a long time, and Putnam explains this in part by pointing to this dense web of free associations in the North versus the barely existent web in the South (Putnam 2000). The northerners used their solid networks to start trading with one another; once they developed friendly social ties, they could use them to develop economic ties, regardless of any state policies. In the South, it was much harder to develop a healthy economy, since there was so little trust between isolated family-based clans. To this day, the North has a healthier economy and more abun-dant civic life than the South. Therefore, Putnam concludes, in the Italian case, more civic life lead to more economic growth. The one case works very well, and there are many cases around the world that echo this harmony between civic associations and a strong economy. However, there are also many cases that have not worked that way. China's economy is developing quickly with almost no free associational life, for example.

State and civic life: not a see-saw

The view that sees civic life and state power on a see-saw is inac-curate in another way, as well. There is simply no evidence for it. There is no evidence that volunteers routinely take up the slack when the state recedes. Instead, astonishingly for a typical American, there is some significant evidence that the opposite is true: *some of the highest volunteering rates in the world are in nations that also have a strong, central welfare state.* Those societies – mostly in northern Europe – use their government to ensure that no one becomes too poor or illiterate to live a fully human life. They do not rely on unpaid volunteers and the market to feed the poor family, care for the senior citizen, and provide music lessons to disadvantaged young people: the state uses tax money to provide these goods. The "Anglo-Saxon countries" – that is, the UK, USA, Australia, New Zealand, and to a lesser extent, Canada – are on the other end of the spectrum.

These strong welfare states do not crush civic engagement. Thus,

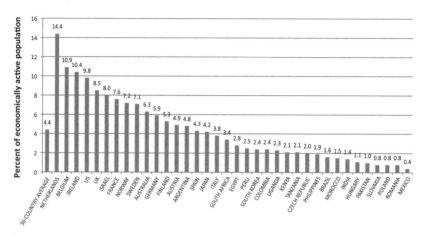

Figure 3.1   Civil society organization workforce as a share of the economically active population in 36 countries, 1995-2000

Source: Salamon & Sokolowski 2004

as shown in Figure 3.1, we find that the nations with the highest civic engagement rates between 1995 and 2000 were the Netherlands, Belgium, Ireland, the USA, the UK, Israel, France, Norway, Sweden, and Australia. The bottom five were Mexico, Romania, Poland, Slovakia, and Pakistan (Salamon and Sokolowski 2004).

Five of the top ten highest countries have strongly redistributive welfare states. We cannot know, from this chart, whether a strong welfare state *causes* more volunteering, but we can know that it does not crush it (Salamon and Sokolowski 2005). But since the USA, UK, Ireland, Israel, and Australia are also near the top of this chart, it is clear that a strong welfare state is not a precondition of high volunteering rates, either.

What about in US history? Has more taxpayer provision of welfare led to less civic volunteering? No, within the United States as well, civic engagement has grown at the same moments that government spending on welfare has grown (Skocpol and Fiorina 1999). US tax rates were at their highest in the mid twentieth century (National Taxpayers Union 2012; Klein 2012; Garofolo 2011), which is also when civic engagement rates were, by some measures, at their highest (Putnam 2000). Again, while this does not demonstrate that the strong welfare state *caused* more civic engagement, it does show that it did not crush it, either. In this chapter and the next, we will, however, see that there are good reasons to assume that more government spending in certain forms does indeed *cause* more civic engagement.

If there *were* a trade-off between civic engagement and a centralized government that promotes class equality, one would expect Sweden to have had low civic engagement during all these years of having a strong welfare state, but it has not. It has had some of the highest rates of civic engagement in the world. If there were such a trade-off, one would expect the era of American history that came close to having a strong welfare state to be the low point of civic engagement. But that era, the mid twentieth century, when taxes on the wealthy were highest, was also the highest point of civic engagement.

On the other side of the coin, there is little evidence pointing toward the opposite hypothesis: that high levels of inequality squelch civic engagement. It is true that most of the world's most highly engaged societies are those egalitarian Northern European countries. However, if inequality unequivocally crushed civic engagement, one would expect the USA to have extremely low civic engagement compared to other developed nations, since a recent CIA survey found that the USA came in 42nd most inegalitarian out of 135 nations (first place for inequality went to Namibia) (https://www.cia.gov/library/publications/the-world-factbook/rankorder/2172rank.html#top). But the USA does not have extremely low levels of civic engagement. One might guess another possible causal relationship: perhaps high levels of inequality provoke activism and rebellion, especially if the society had previously been egalitarian, and the gap between rich and poor has suddenly increased so that many people are suddenly downwardly mobile. This is true sometimes (Merton 1938), but often, high levels of inequality just provoke discouragement. There are very few clear-cut ideas of what social conditions cause civic engagement (partly because of measurement problems to be discussed in a few pages), but one thing is clear: there is not a see-saw relationship between state welfare and civic engagement.

71

Why Does the Idea of the Inverse Relationship Not Die, Then?

Why do politicians keep reviving this argument about the inverse relationship between government and civic engagement, then? Their argument takes up two of the "Right-wing" pieces of Tocqueville. One is the idea that laws can never accomplish what customs can; people need "habits of the heart" as much as laws to keep democracy afloat. Tocqueville did, indeed, say this. But he never imagined that laws and policies would be unnecessary conditions for democracy; rather, he said good laws created necessary but insufficient conditions for democracy.

The second piece of Tocqueville that the politicians have absorbed is the idea that a rising tide raises all boats. When Tocqueville viewed the America of the 1830s, he saw a land of independent farmers, carefully cultivating their own gardens. He stood on the banks of the Ohio River glancing back and forth between the free North and the slave South, and saw that in the North, Americans honored hard work, and their hard work made the land itself more productive. Seeing so palpably that people work harder when they know they will reap what they sow, and seeing that such independent farmers have nothing to fear when they speak out, Tocqueville extolled a system in which no one is an employer or employee, but each owns and controls his own land. With this self-employed citizen in mind, Tocqueville observes the danger of giving over the direct control of the land to a centralized state.

We can see at least part of this process verified in the former Soviet Union, in which big so-called "collective," industrial farms were not very productive per square inch, when compared to each family's tiny, private kitchen garden. Just to clarify a possible misunderstanding: the collective Soviet farms had no resemblance to the grassroots, democratically organized collectives that Emma Goldman described in Spain. Soviet workers had little or no control over production in their big collective farms. From their kitchen gardens, in contrast, they knew they could keep all the carrots and beets they grew, so they toiled diligently in them (Orlov 2008). They also made sure to invest their time and energy wisely in their kitchen gardens, though they often shirked and wasted energy when they were working on the factory farms.

Markets and market competition are indispensable elements of a complex society. This is part of a much bigger argument about how well markets work to assign value in a way that reflects real inputs (there are many shelves of economics texts devoted to this issue, which is discussed from one specific angle at the end of this chapter), but for many items, a market is the best mechanism for assigning value. Without a market, it would be hard to know whether to use tin or silver to make a can, for example, since there would be no easy way of knowing how hard it was to come by the one versus the other.

Our question here is about how to think about how this piece of the social puzzle fits into the bigger picture, with the state and civic associations. From the image of the independent farmers, Tocqueville concludes that economic growth and a flourishing democracy go together. Independent producers work hard to raise everyone's income, so that a rising tide raises all boats; and these independent producers can fearlessly and voluntarily link up in associations, since they are not economically dependent on a big employer.

However, conditions have changed in the USA and other capitalist nations since Tocqueville's day. Independent farmers do not till the land any more. Giant agri-businesses pay low-wage farm-workers to do it. Tocqueville's other fear – the rise of an "aristocracy of industry" that can make workers into mere commodities and abandon workers in hard times – seems more realistic right now. In this situation, many observers of rural economies say that the balance has tipped very far toward "market," with the state bolstering the market, in the USA, by giving huge subsidies to agri-business companies. Like Tocqueville, they might say that now, more of a specific kind of "state" power is needed, not to continue to bolster agricultural corporations' wealth but to help small farmers, reinvigorating democracy by restoring some degree of equality.

The Dangers of Centralized Planning of Big Development Projects

There is, however, still a big piece of Tocqueville's argument regarding the dangers of central planning that is relevant today. There is a long history of massive development plans gone spectacularly wrong when distant experts ignored local people's grassroots wisdom and dreamed up big projects when littler ones might have been better. Whether the centralized decision-making is conducted by states or corporations, the tragic results are sometimes similar.

Two examples drive home the point, standing in for thousands of others: One often-mentioned case of government experts' spectacularly misguided knowledge was the Pruitt-Igoe apartments in St Louis, along with similarly harsh, bleak cement block apartment complexes existing worldwide. Pruitt-Igoe was demolished in 1972, deemed unlivable (Harvey 1990; and you can watch the demolition, in splendid slow motion with trance-like music, in the film Koyonasqaatsi). Massive state-funded projects like this replaced the comfortable blend of ramshackle houses, grocery stores, and schools, which distant experts thought looked disorganized and dirty. It turns out that mixed-use housing was actually good for neighborhoods. Experts finally came to recognize this in the 1990s, after they had already demolished the blocks of old Victorian houses and tree-lined streets. So, the experts now did an about-face, and started promoting "mixed use" housing developments that imitated the neighborhoods that the earlier experts had destroyed!

When the central decision-maker is a large corporation instead of a government, the problem is different, because in addition to the problem of distant, disconnected expertise, there is always the suspicion that the distant experts are making excuses for distant profit-makers to get rich at the local people's expense. From distant corporate headquarters, the message comes that oil companies, mining, or logging companies' technologies are clean and harmless, for example. Local protesters often say that the experts are not just arrogant, but lying. Advocates of mountaintop removal, for example, claim that when they remove entire mountaintops for mining, the resulting runoff and dust is safe for humans, good for the forests, and good for the local economy (cited in Perks 2009). Critics, in contrast, say that the distant experts are simply lying, that they are just company shills, railroading decision-making to provide a hygienic mask behind which the corporation can make more money. A related type of centralized decision-making on the part of private companies is the one that Tocqueville described in his "aristocracy of industry" scenario. In that scenario, the experts are not physically distant, but a handful of elites is making decisions that affect everyone else.

Centralized decision-making on the part of big corporations appears, to "common sense," to be so normal and natural, we rarely notice it as a form of central decision-making, even when it permanently alters big parts of the planet, removing mountaintops, spilling oil, or emptying oceans of fish. We tend to worry more about centralized decision-making when states do it than when corporations do it, partly because we just don't see it when the corporations do it. The idea that these decisions should be made privately, in corporate headquarters, by those who have the resources to make them, seems to be part of "common sense," normal and natural.

While the problems of centralized power differ in many crucial ways when they come from market instead of from state experts, there is one similar result related to local civic associational life: the centralized decision-making can take decision-making out of local people's hands, and the distant experts might ignore local sources of knowledge if the knowledge runs counter to the distant experts' knowledge. If informal, local, grassroots knowledge exceeds distant experts' knowledge, the distant experts undermine the local knowledge that was in play. If local people had had more of a say in planning, the result, say critics – whether of distant government planning or distant corporate manipulation of local life – would have been cheaper in the long run, better, and arrived at in a more democratic way.

The lesson has been that giving too much power to distant planners to alter whole environments without local people's active decision-making can be a mistake. More involvement from civic associations could have averted such disasters. In fact, in some cities, it did. In New Haven, Connecticut, to take just one example among many, a spur of a highway just suddenly ends, smack at the spot where grassroots activists in the 1960s simply brought experts' demolition of the local neighborhood to a halt. In other words, local civic associations protected the remaining cityscape from the distant experts' bad plans. To respond to the bad planning, for a short while in the USA at the end of the 1960s, the government policy was "maximum feasible participation" (though, parenthetically, this program soon met its demise, when the local folks' demands became too politically radical for the government to tolerate – poor people wanted health care and more school funding and better paying jobs, not just little niceties; thus, the program quickly was cut, and a title of a book about it [Moynihan 1970] called the short-lived program 'maximum feasible misunderstanding')."

Civic involvement in planning can be crucially important; the question is, again, how to balance the jobs that civic associations can do with the jobs that the state or market can do best. While expert-based central planning of big, ambitious projects can result in disasters like the Pruitt-Igoe or mountaintop removal, we should not automatically assume that all expert-based planning will do so (Schudson 2006). We should not, for example, assume that the routine provision of basic rights to food, housing, education, and health care will also result in disaster, especially considering that the demands for them have come from civic associations in the first place. The disaster that Right-wing theorists and policy-makers imagine emerging from the provision of welfare is that they expect it to weaken civic associations' informal mutual aid (cited voluminously in Beem 1999). However, as noted earlier, when we examine the factual basis of this fear, we find that there is none.

Still, for people in the many so-called Anglo-Saxon nations, it may seem obvious that the route to all good things is the market. Our "common sense" tells us that the way to promote democracy is to promote economic growth, and the way to promote economic growth is to give unregulated, lavish rewards to people who are smart enough, able-bodied enough, and energetic enough to make money, and to encourage local volunteers to take up the slack, voluntarily feeding the hungry and helping out in ghetto schools. The combination of market and freely given civic volunteering will, we assume, make the central government shrink, while preserving and expanding the pure volunteer spirit. One of sociology's greatest missions is to inspect everyday "common sense," and approach it with reason rather than faith. Sometimes, it is really impressive just *how* wrong common sense can be.

The Welfare State, "Social Citizenship," and Democracy

A "welfare state" is one in which the government takes responsibility for the needy (elderly, young, students, ill, mentally ill, etc.) and treats their well-being as a right. In a welfare state, all citizens share more than the abstract equality that the law offers. They also share *"social citizenship:"* the "right" to have basic needs met. Different societies define these needs differently, but they at least include access to health care, housing, food, and education. How good the health care is, and how advanced the education will be, varies from nation to nation. In the USA, education is free only through high school. In most of Europe, in contrast, a university education has been considered a "right" and is therefore free for the student. All taxpayers contribute to this good, so that the whole society can benefit from an educated workforce, and can make use of all students' talents, even students who were not born into well-off families. In the USA, in contrast, such students often simply can not attend college. Welfare states vary in their commitment to providing all citizens with easy access to the society's bounties.

At the beginning of the twentieth century, many scholars predicted that *all* democracies would become "welfare states." They thought that true democracy had to include not just political and legal equality, but some degree of social equality. Steven Rathgeb Smith and Michael Lipsky summarize these writers' ideas. These writers believed that:

... private charity was inconsistent, unreliable, and parochial; thus, the state needed to assume the responsibility for the distribution of services through a state bureaucracy of professional workers who would distribute social welfare services as an entitlement rather than a gift." (Smith and Lipsky 1995: 15)

A couple of assumptions here would be rather uncontroversial, even to people in those "Anglo-Saxon" nations that tend to lack a strong welfare state. One is that private, personal charity can feel degrading to the recipient. Maimonides, a medieval philosopher, said that charity is better when it is anonymous on both sides, neither aggrandizing the giver nor degrading the receiver, but working impersonally. Depersonalizing charity opens the window to the insight that all gifts are gifts from, and to, God. Anonymous charity seems more harmonious with the kind of aid that an impersonal state agency could give than the kind that a face-to-face, individual volunteer could.

Another uncontroversial assumption in the quote above is that private charity can be unreliable and fickle. It depends on givers' whim and on fads: maybe AIDS one year, homelessness the next, Ethiopia the third. If a movie star discovers that cute baby seals are endangered, seals become a big charity issue. If no movie star befriends endangered ugly beetles, they just become extinct even if they are just as important for an ecosystem as the cute, big-eyed seals.

There is one assumption in the idea of the welfare state, however, that might deeply threaten Anglo-Saxon's most cherished assumptions. The idea of "social citizenship" is that mere *legal* equality is not enough to make true democracy possible; beyond legal equality, a degree of economic equality is needed. Anatole France, a nineteenth-century writer, makes the point the fastest in a quip: "The law, in its majestic equality, forbids the rich as well as the poor to sleep under bridges, to beg in the streets, and to steal bread." Whether the law treats the rich and poor as equal, we know they are not.

As noted earlier, Scandinavian countries work hardest to make sure that universal rights are met, whereas the "Anglo-Saxon" nations leave more up to the market, with the USA at the far extreme (Esping-Andersen 1990). The result is that while all of these societies are modern capitalist democracies, they vary dramatically in their levels of poverty. 29 percent of the aged lived in poverty in the UK in the mid 1980s, 24 percent in the USA, 11 percent in Germany, and less than 1 percent in Sweden. Similar differences existed in the poverty rates among families with young children (Esping-Anderson 1990: 57). Since the 1950s, the discrepancy between the Nordic countries and the USA has grown even more, as the USA has become more and more inegalitarian. The gap between the top one percent and the rest of the American population has grown tremendously since the 1950s within the USA. While all of these societies fit into the general category of "capitalist democracies," they distribute the goods of "social citizenship" differently.

Still, we all share the idea that people have rights, and that it is society's duty to protect those rights. How did this idea of rights arise and expand so enormously? Some people argue that the focus on rights is part of the collapse of civic life; when people call something a "right," they imply that it is not negotiable. Civic life should, according to this line of thought, have taught them to negotiate. For this line of thought, the expansion of "rights talk" is a symptom of an inflated welfare state that solves problems bureaucratically and legalistically, instead of by leaving room for the free exchange of ideas (Glendon 1991).

A different explanation sees the expansion of the idea of "rights" as part of society's progress. Rights have been around in various forms for a long time. Many religious traditions, and all societies that have laws, include some vague idea of rights. The Bible, for example, says that after seven years, all debts must be forgiven and all servants freed. When we read, "But if your servant says to you: 'I do not want to leave you,' because he loves you and your family and is well off with you, then take an awl and push it through his ear into the door, and he will become your servant for life" (Deuteronomy 15:17), it is a way of branding him, declaring his welfare to be your obligation, as is the welfare of the cattle you have stamped with your insignia. He has what we would now call the "right" not to be abandoned after he has served you for seven years. So there were rights in antiquity, though now, we might not prefer to be nailed to a doorpost.

However, before the nineteenth century, it would have been hard for even an optimistic utopian science fiction writer to imagine including material well-being as a right. As societies became less plagued by famine, hunger, and sickness over the course of the 1800s, more of the bounties of life came to be seen as rights (Marshall 1998 [1958]). With the rise of the factory, people started becoming more productive per hour. In one hour, a person could produce what had once taken three days to produce. Machines could do the toiling, freeing up time for humans to develop themselves the way only the wealthy had done before this era. It started to seem obvious a hundred years ago that *some day soon*, we could *all* fairly easily have our basic needs met, with very little back-breaking labor. New-found powers to manage predictable risks added to this impression that humans could get fear off their backs. If, for example, the invention of antibiotics meant that no child had to die of a minor infection, it started to feel like a crime not to prevent the death, *even if* the child's parents could not afford it. Utopian novels (Gilman 1979 [1915]; Butler 1872; Huxley 1962) and political pamphlets – most notably, Marx's Communist Manifesto – spell out this constellation of hopes.

When those hopeful people of the nineteenth and twentieth centuries imagined their future, they imagined a time when no one would be so plagued by fear of hunger, homelessness, and curable diseases that they could not go forward, to think about more abstract, large-scale issues. Slowly, it started to seem as if desperate need would soon no longer loom over anyone's life; as if everyone could realistically have enough in "the affluent society" (Galbraith 1967). It was "the end of scarcity" (Gorney 1972). If everyone could have "enough," could spend less time toiling and could let machines do the work, then real democracy could be possible, *for the first time in history. For the first time in history*, it started to look as though people could stop spending most of their days worrying about the next meal, and could start to do the thing that only humans are capable of doing: planning their own societies together, consciously, on purpose.

Why didn't the past's rosy future come true? Tocqueville predicted one reason: while technology grew more and more powerful, control of the economy grew concentrated in fewer and fewer hands. Surprisingly, marvelous inventions did not give more people more time to participate in decision-making about how to run society. Instead, in bad times, it led to lay-offs and poverty. In good times, it led to a seemingly endless production of new "needs," so that nothing was "enough" and people stayed harnessed to the treadmill of work (Schor 1992). This glimmer of hope in this abundant future nonetheless remains, in many social movements – not just in the yellowed pages of utopian novels. It remains, but often in a less simple, utopian form, and instead, in a careful consideration of a balance between market, state, and civic life, so that a society's social tripod tips more toward civic and state, and leans less heavily and less exclusively on "market."

The Strange Case of Missing Social Citizenship in the USA

The USA has, of all wealthy nations, leaned most heavily toward valuing the market and civic associations, and distrusting the state. From the nation's beginnings, its founders argued that while other nations were held together by blood and roots, civic associations should be the glue that held Americans together (Hendrickson 2010).

Paradoxically, though, civic associations soon turned around and fought to make the state grow, by pressing for government protection of women and children, widows and veterans. If we count unions as "civic associations," then even more of the state was a product of civic associations' pressure to protect the disadvantaged, when they fought for the weekend, the eight hour workday, workplace safety, and the rest of the state regulations aimed at protecting workers from the excesses of the market.

The first big *welfare* program, giving direct hand-outs to the needy, was for Civil War veterans. They were treated as a special case that deserved government aid and protection. However, there was no policy of universal benefits for all old, sick people, so when those veterans died, the policy died, too (Skocpol 1995). Remarkably, women's groups met more success when they fought for welfare for mothers and children – even before women had the right to vote! Many of the active proponents of government spending on child welfare were women who had started their careers as volunteers. These successful activists got their know-how in settlement houses like Jane Addams' Hull House and in other local clubs that were linked together into national associations (this whole tale is told in Skocpol [1995: 342]). This mutual back-and-forth between civic associations and government enhanced the allure of civic associations, by making the power of association so visible. Because of these associations' power, a small welfare state started to develop in the USA. Still, the USA was an outlier in its lack of "social citizenship."

When working people could not find jobs during the Great Depression of 1929, private charities could no longer keep up with the flood of demands. At the same time, a massive drought, the "Dust Bowl" of the 1920s and 1930s, added to the population of poor, homeless, unemployed workers and their families. Before these simultaneous crises, there was a jumble of private charities, sometimes randomly getting some city or state aid. The central government almost never funded any disaster relief (Clemens 2010). After the Great Depression and the Dust Bowl, though, it got harder to "blame the victims," by saying that these social and ecological disasters were workers' and farmers' and their families' fault, or by saying that to pull themselves out of poverty, the workers, farmers, and their children simply had to work harder.

Even so, amidst the tent cities of unemployed workers camped out in front of the White House, and the flocks of Dust Bowl refugees, there was still another reason to deny them government aid. President Hoover was still extolling the virtue-producing effects of private charity, saying,

> ... if we break down this sense of responsibility and individual generosity ... and we start appropriations ... we have not only impaired

something infinitely valuable in the life of the American people, we have struck at the roots of self-government. (Clemens 2010: 88)

Finally, reluctantly, the federal government started to help the victims of the Depression and the Dust Bowl.

The provisional solution that simultaneously addressed Hoover's fears of centralized government, while also trying to meet people's basic needs, was to funnel government funds *through* private charities like the Red Cross. The word for this is "outsourcing." When a government "outsources," it means that it hires outside, non-governmental providers of the goods or services. Usually, they are nonprofits, and that means they involve volunteers. The goal of this "outsourcing" has been to preserve local decision-making and the spirit of voluntarism, while *also* ensuring "social citizenship." Providing this aid meant that government spending rose.

During the New Deal era, the pendulum swung slightly toward a stronger state in other, more direct ways, as well, and this continued through the 1970s. The highways that crisscross the country, dams to provide electricity, and military research that eventually led to the invention of the internet: the federal government funded them. Public libraries and school libraries, health care, higher education, housing, food, playgrounds, parks and public pools, help for the disabled and elderly: all of these started to seem possible to provide for everyone. In the 1950s, the distribution of income was much flatter than it is today, and taxes on the wealthy were much higher than they are today, as noted earlier. The set of rights grew. But there were still big arguments about the proper role of government funding. Around this same time, some Right-wing legislators resurrected the fear that a "welfare state" was looming too close on our horizon (Smith and Lipsky 1995), though surprisingly, it was a former general and Republican, Dwight D. Eisenhower, who was President when much of this government expansion occurred.

Remember, throughout this brief history, that Hoover was wrong about the inverse relationship between volunteering and government involvement. While one of our most dearly held beliefs about centralized government is, therefore, incorrect, it has, nonetheless, steered a great deal of social policy.

Government spending rose till the 1980s (Smith and Lipsky 1995). The idea, once again, was that since local nonprofits seem to be closer to the ground than distant government experts, we could have our cake and eat it, too. We could have some degree of equality ensured by the state with its superior financial resources (the cake), and also have decentralized decision-making (eat it, too). Since much of this money was funneled through local nonprofits, the nonprofit sector grew, enlisting many volunteers. This helps explain a puzzle we noticed earlier: that the relation between government spending and volunteering is not an inverse one. When the government funnels money through nonprofits, and the nonprofits have to enlist volunteers in order to retain their nonprofit status (which the nonprofits must do to qualify as nonprofits, according to USA tax code), then government spending leads to more volunteering.

Even with this decentralization, some policy-makers and voters panicked, fearful that they were becoming infants in the nanny state. The "Reagan Revolution" in the early 1980s slashed spending. Meanwhile, many nonprofits had come to rely on the mid century's high tide of state spending (Smith and Lipsky 1993). So when the high tide receded in the 1980s and 1990s, many nonprofits were left high and dry, scrambling for funds, laying off employees, cutting services, and leaving volunteers with too much responsibility for them to handle.

The Tocquevillean balance had tipped back again, away from government funding, and toward market solutions to social problems. Whereas in the 1950s, the top one percent of the population earned eight percent of the nation's income, by 2004, the top one percent of the population was making almost a quarter of the income. The middle class was disappearing, and the schools, libraries, parks, public universities, and public swimming pools started shrinking, drying up, closing down. The dream of social citizenship in the USA seemed dead. Cutting back on government was supposed to lead to more civic engagement. Perhaps it did, but in a way that policy-makers had not intended.

Occupy Wall Street, Arab Spring, Greek Rebellion: Another Balance

Perhaps 2011 opened a new chapter in the wobbly balance between grassroots participation and market. The world exploded in grassroots protests against growing inequality and a growing tendency worldwide to put most of a society's eggs in the basket of "the market," and hardly any in the state. The Occupy and indignados' movements around the world, Arab Spring's rebellions all over the Arab world, and less populous but equally remarkable rebellions elsewhere forced the world to ask how the "free" market is not free. Some of Occupy Wall Street's first website page entries were protesting the deregulation of the US stock market; the repeal of the then-obscure Glass-Steagal Act that had regulated banking since the New Deal till its repeal in 1999. The movement also protested government regulators' serving on the Boards of Directors of the banks they were supposed to regulate (see "Occupy Wall Street Forum Post," September, 28, 2011 for example; see also Ketcham 2011).

Another example of the mutual back scratching between market and state, to which the Occupy movement has drawn attention, concerns the worldwide subsidies of oil, coal, and gas, instead of alternative energy. In recent years, governments held down the cost of fossil fuels by using subsidies. In the USA, tax money went to this, instead of, for example, paying for things like university education. Worldwide, the subsidies added up to between 45 billion and 75 billion dollars per year in recent years (Gurria 2011). Consumers take the price into account, and this price is heavily subsidized by automatic, forced payments in the form of taxes. Consumers' "choices" to drive rather than take the bus, or to cool an office building with coal-powered electricity rather than installing solar panels or opening the windows, are based on prices that do not reflect the real cost of fossil fuels. These are not "free market" choices. As the OECD – not exactly a radical activist organization (it's a data-gathering agency) – said, if the prices were more realistic, we would drive less and produce fewer greenhouse gasses (Gurria 2011). What looks like a "free" market, here and elsewhere as well, is, the Occupy Movement activists said, really a government-subsidized market.

In these and many other ways, people around the world were starting to lose their tight grip on "market fundamentalism" – the near-religious faith that the market can solve all problems. Perhaps in the balance between market, state, and civic association, the balance is starting to tip slightly away from the market. Iceland provided the world with an especially clean example of the problem with handing over a nation's fate to the market. Here is the CIA, also not exactly a fount of Leftist politics, describing Iceland: "Prior to the 2008 crisis, Iceland had achieved high growth, low unemployment, and a remarkably even distribution of income" (https://www.cia.gov/library/publications/the-world-factbook/geos/ ic.html). The CIA document said that Iceland had had abundant green energy, good schools, workers were paid well, and everyone had had time for leisure. Even when viewed from places with milder climates, it could have looked appetizing.

In the 2000s, everything changed: Iceland *deregulated* and *privatized* its banks. There were fewer restrictions on what the banks could do with the money (whether they had to invest it at home, abroad, with what interest rates, and above all, at what levels of risk, for example). The banks were no longer controlled by the government, as they had been previously, but were sold to private entrepreneurs. They were now commercial enterprises – part of the "market." At the height of deregulation, the Icelandic bankers had paid internationally renowned economists to write scholarly articles saying that the deregulation was a success. During these years of the Icelandic "miracle," inequality grew, while government policies shifted more of the tax burden onto the poor. Then, when the banks collapsed, a couple of years later, the ordinary people of Iceland were supposed to pay. Each person in Iceland now owes about $403,000 per person, most of it to the agencies that bailed out the millionaire bankers who speculated with the nation's money (Boyes 2009: 144). In spring of 2011, the bailout was put to a vote. 93 percent of Icelanders voted no (Sigurgeirsdóttir and Wade 2011).

Iceland's case is particularly clear because before this moment of deregulation and privatization, it was one of the world's most solidly prosperous nations, with a solid middle class, strong welfare rights, and virtually no poverty. When the balance tipped way over in favor of the market, it *did* invoke more civic action ... in the form of protest! It was not the innocent, apolitical volunteering that theorists like Putnam expect.

Letting the market rule provoked a backlash from civic associations elsewhere, as well. The International Monetary Fund is a global agency that, among other things, lends money to nations. It has often been accused of extracting money from the poor to pay off loans that ended up in rich people's pockets. As its current head put it,

> We all learned some important lessons from the Arab Spring. While the top-line economic numbers – on growth, for example – often looked good, too many people were being left out. And, speaking for the IMF, while we certainly warned about the ticking time bomb of high youth unemployment in the region, we did not fully anticipate the consequences of unequal access to opportunities. Let me be frank: we were not paying enough attention to how the fruits of economic growth were being shared. (Lagarde 2011)

When the balance goes out of whack between civic, state, and market forces, civic organizations keep popping up to reset it (Polanyi 2011), but these associations are not placid do-gooders who feed the homeless without asking why there is homelessness. They are rebels. In the USA, Greece, Iceland, Spain, Canada, and elsewhere, some grassroots activists are rebelling against the idea that the market can solve everything, and are starting to become political activists, when they "connect the dots."

Two Puzzles of Measurement: "Rates of Civic Association" and "Progress"

This chapter has been devoted to comparisons of civic engagement over time and between nations. It has asked how people in different times and places have struck a balance between civic life, the state, and the market. We need to be able to do this, but since every keyword in politics is a matter of dispute, it should come as no surprise that there are many data sets about the civic sector, each with its own definition of the thing it claims to measure. It should also come as no surprise that measuring how successful the balance is, is also a matter of dispute.

Let's first examine the puzzles of measuring civic engagement. It is very difficult to compare rates of civic engagement across nations, because different researchers include different activities in the category. The trustworthy ones clearly explain their criteria for including and excluding organizations. Consider the case of Finland, and a diligent study of its civic engagement. Surveys of volunteer rates *could* ask about "the nonprofit sector," "the third sector (that is, neither governments nor market)," "the associational sector," "popular movements," "civil society," "the social economy," "the informal sector" (which includes informal cooperation, like parent coop day care, and also includes non-legal market activity like unlicensed street vendors), self-help groups and mutual aid groups like quilting bees and barn-raisings, or activist groups, or all or some of the above. Should the survey include labor unions? What about activist organizations that become political parties and whose members then enter government? Depending on what sorts of organizations one includes, one gets different results. Furthermore, Finnish civic associations – however defined – usually work very closely with local governments, and often get money from them, and membership in some, such as local road-building associations, is mandatory (Helander and Sundback 1998: 18). Another question about the boundaries of "civic" regards religious associations. In Uzbekistan, the mahallah has been acting as a customary Islamic mutual aid society. It endured even during the Soviet era, *minus* the religious aspect, *plus* some heavy dependence on state funding. Then, was that "civic," too, as at least one scholar argues (Makarova 1998)? Here again, it depends on your definition.

One clever cross-national survey asked people what they *themselves* consider to be "volunteering," and the differences in results were striking (Dekker and Halman 2003). In some nations, helping family members was seen as volunteering, and in some, serving as an usher at a concert in order to get free admission was seen as volunteering. Statistics in social science usually work this way: a man who is asked "how many children do you have?" might wonder if we include the ones he has never met, the ones he is pretty sure are his, his step-children, his biological children who are being raised by another father, etc. His answer might be "one" or "eight." The measurement of civic engagement rates depends, as in any scientific endeavor, on the questions that the researcher is asking, and on the respondents' interpretations of those questions.

Measuring progress: is the economy all that counts?

Another measurement puzzle concerns the measurement of a society's overall well-being. To measure a society's overall success, economists and policy-makers usually rely on the Gross Domestic Product as an important indicator. The GDP focuses exclusively on the market, based on the fundamental faith that if the market is doing well, everything is doing well. Here again, social scientists have begun to assert that a better measure of well-being could focus attention on re-aligning the society's axels in a way that strikes a better balance between market, state, civic, and other forces.

The GDP measures the market value of all goods and services produced in a nation in a given period of time. If a nation's GDP is high, most economists and policy-makers up to the twenty-first century would have presumed that its economy is doing well, and that therefore people are doing well. So when Iceland had its first billionaire in 2007, many economists cheered, seeing it as a sign of a growing economy in which "the likelihood of a financial meltdown is low" (Mishkin and Herbertsson 2006: 9, for example). And if it were indeed progress, then the activists of Arab Spring, the Occupy movements, and similar previous activists would be "against progress." But is it progress?

The problem with the GDP is that it only measures how much money changes hands, and averages it out across the whole population. If a great deal of money changes hands so people can buy burglar alarms, fences for their mansions, private security forces, and tranquilizers to soothe the headaches they get from protecting themselves from the poor or from being poor, the economy is doing well, as the GDP measures it. If a few people grow fantastically wealthy, the GDP goes up, even if most people's incomes plunge dramatically. If you hire a nanny, it contributes to the GDP; if you take care of your child yourself, it does not. An hour-long daily commute in a car contributes much more to the GDP than a daily fifteen-minute walk to work. Cleaning up an oil spill is extremely expensive, so that greatly contributes the GDP, too (Stiglitz, Sen, and Fitoussi 2010)!

There are good reasons to assume that measuring the amount of money that has changed hands will not reveal the level of well-being in a society, even for the wealthy. Many studies and data sets show that past a certain point, material well-being does not bring overall well-being (Bok 2011; Easterlin 2010). Americans reported themselves to be happiest in the 1950s, which is also when houses were smaller, people owned fewer cars, worked fewer hours, and the gap between the rich and the poor was much, much smaller. The level of inequality in a society is more harmful to people's well-being than poverty. People of equal material wealth vary in their levels of well-being from one society to another: those in societies with greater inequality have worse physical and mental health, do worse on intelligence tests, and are unhappier, than those who live in societies with a smaller gap between rich and poor (Wilkenson and Pickett 2010). These studies also find that people who lead economically precarious lives are anxious and unhappy, and suffer not just emotionally, but physically, from this stress.

The GDP, like other measurement, does not just "measure," but also works as a powerful symbol. When we symbolize our society's success in the GDP's terms, we organize our society to increase market transactions. We want to make ourselves look better in our mirror, in our collective self-representation. The way we measure success, in other words, steers our aspirations; the measurement helps create the reality it aims to measure; it becomes a kind of deity to whom we make sacrifices.

If our basic faith in civic associations has any truth to it, it rests on the idea that humans can consciously and collectively organize their lives together. Perhaps, then, we could devise a better way of understanding our shared goal, other than "more money changing hands." Canada's head epidemiologist Michael Pennock and Bhutanese planner Dasho Karma Ura have started to develop such a measure: a "Happiness Index" (Pennock and Ura 2007). Another such effort, sponsored by one of the world's most important data-gathering organizations, the Organisation for Economic Cooperation and Development, is in the works (Stiglitz, Sen, and Fitoussi 2010). In the book *Mismeasuring Our Lives*, the authors describe a survey that asks a whole battery of questions aimed at measuring the society's "well-being." The questionnaires would ask, for example, how environmentally sustainable your life is; how much household income you have not just from your own job, but also how much you benefit indirectly from government funding of your health care, schools, parks, and water purification systems; how much suffering you endure from long commutes, air pollution, and high crime rates; how much inequality, job instability, and unemployment ordinary people face; and how happy or anxious you tell the survey researcher you feel. Studies show that part of what makes a society more liveable is that there is room for ordinary citizens to have some civic engagement and to have a political voice, so the survey measures this, as well.

British Prime Minister David Cameron in 2012 started initiating a "happiness" survey. Oddly, his highly stripped-down version only asks, in various forms, how happy or anxious you feel. Critics argue that the project claims to measure happiness while the government's current policies of enthusiastically cutting welfare undermine "happiness," as it is defined in the larger questionnaire. When there are cutbacks in schools and social services, the critics say that it will be harder for people to experience the well-being and "happiness" that comes from "social citizenship" (Al-Daini 2011).

Market fundamentalism

The question this chapter poses for civic associations is, "Which decisions do we want to let people make privately, and which do we want to be up for public discussion and decided democratically?"

While the definitions of "civic association" and "well-being" are under dispute, there are nonetheless a few pieces of data that hold still, across all of the definitions. One is that among the nations with the highest rates of volunteering – however defined – are the Nordic countries, which also have the strongest welfare states and the least inequality. If we in the English-speaking nations do not want central governments to redistribute wealth, we have to look for a new reason why not: *we cannot assume that it will discourage the volunteer spirit.* When we think about designing or participating in volunteer projects or activism, this chapter clearly shows we should not expect a see-saw between volunteering and government. While leaders like Prime Minister Cameron, and the current heads of state in the Netherlands (Duyvendak, Grootegoed and Tonkens forthcoming) are cutting social services, they are also cheering for more volunteering. These leaders are hoping that volunteers will step in when government recedes, and that they will do a better job. As this chapter has shown, that is almost always untrue; more often, government programs create new opportunities for volunteers. As Dame Elisabeth Hoodless, the head of the UK's largest volunteer program put it, "there are a lot of very worthwhile programmes – for example volunteers working in child protection as promoted by the minister for children – which are now under threat of closure" (BBC 2011). Organizing this kind of massive volunteering is a full-time job. When governments cut back, there are fewer, and less effective, places for this kind of volunteering.

Parenthetically, we can add to this upending of common sense: high levels of inequality discourage economic growth, according to many studies (Davis 2004; Klein 2012), so an unfettered market is not even good for the market itself (Polanyi 2001 [1944]). Using John Maynard Keynes' tremendously influential ideas, this was mainstream economists' and business leaders' conclusion during most of the twentieth century: market and state had to work together to keep markets stable, not just to prevent crashes and bloody uprisings, but also, to make it possible for inventors to take small risks without risking everything. Remember one typical, though stellar example: the invention of the internet was originally funded by military research. It was called ARPANET and was a result of heavy government investment, not a free market. To the list of other inventions made possible by US government funding, we can also add "semiconductors, radar . . . the radio, the jet engine and many medical advances, including penicillin" (Leonhardt 2012). In other words, government involvement can, if done well, be very good for economic growth.

If we in the English-speaking nations prefer to let the market rule and create vast inequalities, it is a matter of *principle*. It is not about what the market and inequality *do* to make our lives better. The promise of civic association is that humans can use reason and morality together, to shape their society, consciously. If we know that the existence of a welfare state does not dampen the volunteer spirit, but can promote equality, so that poor children and rich children can have equal chances to soar, why ignore what we know?

"Market fundamentalism" is the term scholars use to describe this near-religious faith in the market. It describes a kind of faith that treats the market not just as the solution to most problems, but also as a good in itself. It seems that the Anglo-Saxon ideal of the near omnipotence of the "free market" works more like a religion – irrefutable with any data, but based on a fundamental faith in the sanctity of the free market – than a practical solution to a problem in this world.

4

─────

Neo-Liberalism and Grassroots Organizations

A Tocquevillean group of the unpaid local folks banding together, outside of any government or commerce, is one kind of civic association, but there are many others. When people think about civic engagement, they often have a jumble of mismatched entities in their heads, and they summarize it all by imagining one model of the civic association: the Tocquevillean ideal. This is a problem, because not all civic associations match that organizational form. It is what linguist anthropologists call "idealized cognitive model" (Lakoff 1987). Think of a fruit. Quick.

Did you think of "zucchini," "avocado," or "raspberry?" Probably not. If one generalized about "fruits" with only "apples" and "oranges" in mind, this would be a problem. People speaking of civic associations might mean an unpaid local Tocquevillean volunteer group, a charity, an activist group, an international NGO, or an NGO that gets government funds to do social service within the USA. All these different "organizational forms" do not all work the same way. We need a more realistic view of civic associations than the Tocquevillean ideal gives.

This chapter will mostly be about an entity which few people have thought much about: the Non-Governmental Organization (often called "nonprofit" in the USA, due to its classification in our tax code).

Many NGOs' budgets are larger than many nations'! Many NGOs overturn government and corporate policies! They did this when, for example, indigenous people in Chiapas in the 1990s

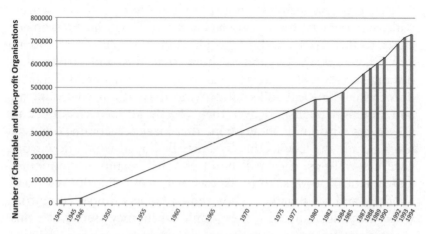

Figure 4.1 Rise in the Number of NGOs in the USA, 1940s–1990s
Data source: Hall 2006, Tables 55–64.

challenged the Mexican government's policies, or Nigerians challenged their government and the Royal Dutch Shell, bypassed local authorities, and appealed to an international humanitarian public.

Within the USA, NGOs employ more people than the entire agricultural sector!

A great deal of activism and volunteering nowadays happens in NGOs. Non-governmental, civic associations have been important in the USA since the beginning, but there has been explosive growth in the non-governmental sector in the past forty years, both in the USA and around the world. People writing about international economic development call it "the rise and rise of NGOs," adding a twist to the usual "rise and fall" image – they just keep going up and up.

As of the late 1990s, there were over one million such organizations in India alone, according to one count, and over 200 thousand in Brazil (Salamon and Anheier 1997). The growth of these organizations worldwide has been exponential (Edwards and Hulme 1996). Yet, these powerful, unelected decision-making bodies do not figure very prominently in our visions of society. Most people have probably never thought about them at all.

A central goal behind this explosive growth in NGOs world-wide over the past forty years has been "to bring the government closer to the people, and the people closer to each other" (Booth and Jouve 2005). Organizers hope that this will ensure that distant experts will no longer plan projects from a great distance, dislocating the local folks, destroying the natural environment, and running roughshod over their locally attuned customs and grassroots wisdom. Planners hope that local decision-making will teach people the lessons that Tocqueville hoped would flow from civic associations: they will build citizens' cognitive, emotional, and practical powers, to think together, feel solidarity with one another, and act together. How these planners' hopes come true when they do, and why they don't when they don't, are this chapter's questions.

What Is an NGO?

There is a great deal of disagreement about what to count as a non-governmental organization (hereafter abbreviated as NGO, and used synonymously with "nonprofit"). One scholarly article calls it "Mission Impossible" (Martens 2002). However, scholars and policy-makers generally use this definition. They:

1 are *organizations,* not just temporary or informal, but have some long-term existence (often, though not necessarily, including president, vice president, secretary etc.);
2 are *separate* from government (though they may receive substantial government funding);
3 *are not mainly aimed at generating profit* for the CEOs;
4 *are self-governing,* rather than being fully controlled by outside entities;
5 use some *volunteers;*
6 serve some *public good,* for *public* benefit, not just selling a commodity for private consumption.
(Salamon and Anheier 1996)

There are many kinds of NGOs. Despite the "non-governmental" piece of the definition, many NGOs blend government funds with private funds, and many work so closely with government, they are not really independent. In some countries – most notably, China (Spires 2011) – the government keeps them on such a tight leash and under such close surveillance, scholars call most of them Governmental Non-Governmental Organizations, otherwise known as "GONGOs"!

There are, thus, several *slight problems* with this definition. By this definition, Harvard, Greenpeace, most soup kitchens, museums, preschools, symphony orchestras, mental health clinics, and hospitals could fit (Salamon and Anheier 1996: 11). So, why do we have the category "NGO" at all? If it is so nebulous, shouldn't we get rid of it?

Here, we need another short detour into sociolinguistics, regarding the nature of language in general(!) All important social categories are like this one: magnets for argument, constellations of debate. We need them precisely because they crystallize our debates and allow us to argue about the entities that invoke the most passion in us. Philosophers like Ludwig Wittgenstein add that *all* words are like that. We need nebulous categories like "family," "school," and "NGO." We use them, and in informal, everyday conversation, we know how to use them and make sense of them. We can't define them. We know how to use these nebulous categories, and we have to pin them down for legal arguments, such as attributing paternity to a father who should pay a child's bills. We need precise definitions for law and for policy, but no single definition will satisfy all purposes. In everyday usage, the vague ones work better. If you say, "my choral group is my 'family,'" we know what that means, but as a legal statement, it would be untrue. No matter how many pages of fine print one adds onto the legal statement (think of your annual credit-card policy statements), no single definition will cover all cases. We now return to less philosophical issues.

Civic associations in the USA have never uniformly matched the Tocquevillean ideal to begin with, as noted in the previous chapter. Now, there are even more ways that current civic engagement is different from that image. Much civic action happens in organizations with paid employees, a budget, funders, national or international participants, and in organizations that are in many other ways different from little local face-to-face volunteer groups. These NGOs are this chapter's topic.

Organizations take different routes to becoming an NGO, some of which get government money. One route to becoming an NGO starts when a government program gets outsourced to volunteers who may work with a few paid professionals – many mental health agencies, and worker training programs in the USA started this way, for example. A second sort of NGO arises when a volunteer group or activist group grows successful enough to get donations, hire a few people, and register as a more formal entity with its own bank account and legal identity, rather than just a completely informal group or network. Among these is a third possible type: those that get government funds, as opposed to just getting donations from private sources. Of course, there still are also some purely voluntary, local, Tocquevillean civic associations, but to highlight the fact that there are some important differences between them and the more formal organizations with paid employees, we will not call those Tocquevillean groups "NGOs."

Empowerment Projects

The rest of this chapter will focus on a large *subset* of NGOs: those that aim to "empower" people, and use what you could call "empowerment talk." They call for engagement that blends many missions:

Civic self-help, being open, egalitarian, voluntary, helping the volunteer by making him/her responsible;
Innovation, being deeply challenging, inspiring, multicultural, aimed at getting you to "break out of your box" and to "stretch your comfort zone,'" personally transformative;
Hands-on, appreciation of unique people and cultures, commu-

nity-based, local, natural, grassroots, not based on distant, abstract expert knowledge;

Transparency to many distant, hurried sponsors, easily accountable on a short time-line;

Helping the needy without being "charity."

This subset of NGOs, which we can call "empowerment projects," tend to develop a predictable set of tensions (Eliasoph 2011). Let's first look closely at some examples, to glimpse some of the variations in how this organizational form works. The studies used here to illustrate these tensions can easily stand in for dozens of similar studies, and probably for thousands of similar cases around the world.

A big *proviso*: Some NGOs are not empowerment projects. Many NGOs' whole purpose is to awaken concern about a political controversy, and to get new policies in place. On the Left and on the Right, thousands of NGOs around the world try to educate the public about their vision of social problems. These projects are not empowerment projects if they do not have all the crisscrossed missions that empowerment projects have. We will come back to this near the end of the chapter.

Tension 1: Civic self-help versus helping the needy

Around the world, many NGOs have a mission of using civic engagement as a kind of *self-help*. Civic engagement, according to this approach, teaches people how to make responsible decisions. Civic actors also are said to learn specific skills like note-taking and chairing a meeting (Verba, Schlozman, and Brady 1996). Volunteering is supposed to build character. That is part of why many of these programs get funded. This character and skill-building mission often goes with the mission of lifting participants out of poverty.

Programs like these need to show that they are on the road to sustainability, and this means getting the recipients of aid to take responsibility for their own recovery. I first noticed this problem when I was doing the research for *Making Volunteers* (Eliasoph

2011), studying after-school programs for disadvantaged youth, the adult volunteers who helped in those programs, and the youth volunteer projects in which after-school program members participated. This was in a mid-sized city, Snowy Prairie, in the United States in the early 2000s. There, this tangle meant that even disabled senior citizens had to show that they were not just getting a hand-out, but were active and peppy volunteers. When the head of the program for disabled senior citizens learned that this would be the new empowering approach taken by the United Way, a large, umbrella nonprofit that distributed donations to smaller nonprofits that were under its wing, she broke down in tears.

A related puzzle with this mixture is that participants in these programs often are unsure if they are the givers, the recipients, or both. Are the organizations promoting "civic volunteering" so that the volunteers can help needy others? Or are the volunteers supposed to be helping themselves? Who's the problem? Here for example, a reporter was interviewing some youth volunteers who were helping out at a local event. He asked a question that was intended to give a boy a chance to display his generous volunteer spirit:

Reporter: Why are you here today?

Wispy black boy, maybe fourteen years old: I'm involved instead of being out on the streets or instead of taking drugs or doing something illegal. (Eliasoph 2011: 17)

The wispy boy's response was not *quite* a mistake. He was a participant in a "prevention program" for "at-risk youth." He understood that for a teen like him, volunteering is supposed to make HIM a responsible person, and, in that way, lift *him* out of poverty. Teens in these programs were constantly being told that they could make a difference, in their own lives as well as the lives of others, as long as they made the right "choices." But what if his problem is that he lacks something other than good character, self-esteem, and a *feeling* of responsibility? What if the wispy boy lacks something that is frankly more expensive than self-esteem?

For example, what if his parents have to work two jobs to make ends meet, and there is no one available to help him with homework? Or what if he has a paid job to help pay his family's rent, and has to babysit his younger siblings, because his parents can't afford day care?

This tension plays out all over the world. A clear example comes from a Danish aid worker who is charged with distributing funds to fledgling civic associations in Albania, the poorest country in Europe (Sampson 1996). Steven Sampson's mission is to promote civic engagement as a form of self-help. The idea is based on the Tocquevillean assumption that a country with more local, grassroots civic associations will have a better economy *and* more grassroots democracy. Albania will, according to this rationale, get economic development because the people will develop "social capital," as they learn to trust one another, to see how investing in shared goods like highways and schools will benefit everyone, even if each person does not benefit individually from every shared investment. Neighborhood A will agree, for example, to pave a mile's worth of streets in Neighborhood B's neighborhood one year, if Neighborhood A is sure that Neighborhood B across town will vote for paving the streets in the A neighborhood the next year.

Sampson is supposed to help needy Albanians. To develop the economy, however, his program is based on the philosophy that just giving needy people money, food, and medicine will not solve long-term problems. Many of us have seen the inspirational poster with this slogan on them: "If you give a man a fish, he eats for a day. If you teach a man to fish, he eats for a lifetime." Sampson's mission is to "teach the man to fish," of course (see also Swidler and Watkins 2009). The Albanians need to learn to make effective decisions together and to take responsibility, and his mission is to fund the kinds of civic associations that will do that.

Being a thoughtful fellow, however, Sampson notices some problems. His well-intentioned aid inadvertently gives privilege to those who are already privileged, and undermines the traditional associations that already existed – when it neglects the already-existing association of village elders!

There is "a gap between those groups led by young, Anglophone, well-travelled intellectuals and others whose members were less articulate and more isolated. The first group, including youth, environmental, women's and human-rights groups, often had wide-ranging public-service projects; they knew the language of projects and had often been to seminars abroad. The second group, older, Albanian-speaking and unfamiliar with the world of projects, tended to focus on increased social services, entitlements, or payments for their constituents. They included groups for aiding orphans, hemophiliacs, veterans, the handicapped, disabled workers, pensioners, and the political-prisoners group. (Sampson 1996: 134)

For long-term purposes, funding organizations that look like they will develop the economy makes sense, but the village elders, disabled veterans, and hemophiliacs need the fish *right now*. They might *never* learn to fish. Furthermore, while these civil society projects have to "empower women," as the lingo holds, the village elders rarely express interest in combating sexism. In contrast, while the cool, urban, computer-savvy, cosmopolitan elites in the first group may or may not be very interested in combating sexism either, they know how to put on a good show of it. The result is perverse:

Not knowing the 'culture' of projects, many of these older NGO members place the emphasis on getting money, rather than on their ideas for projects or the goals of their organization . . . Albanians who have computers and internet access, who know how to speak project-speak, and who can network, interpersonally, with the NGO officials tend to get money from NGOs; the old rural folks who had previously been the informal leaders of local life tend to lose out. (Sampson 1996: 136)

Whether in Albania or Snowy Prairie, the local people who are relatively literate and slightly better off often win the foreign NGOs' grants. They start to climb the social ladder. There is a high risk that they will leave the less literate, worse-off folks behind. In Malawi, the people who can learn to move gracefully in the world of foreign NGOs become a new elite (Swidler 2006;

Swidler and Watkins 2006, 2009). Since paid positions as movers and shakers in the local NGO network are rare, there is a hidden personal tragedy here. As word spreads about this route out of poverty, unrealistic hopes soar. Young women in Malawi start to *believe* the hopeful language of projectspeak, saying that if they focus on their studies, they can do anything. Keep your eyes on the prize. Some forsake marriage and forsake making more realistic plans. They are left high and dry when their unrealistic hopes do not materialize (Frye forthcoming).

Micro-finance is another approach that blends these missions. The micro-finance movement began in the late 1970s in India, with the goal of empowering poor would-be entrepreneurs – often, women, in particular – by giving them small, low-interest loans. Normal banks usually refuse loans to such poor people, because the risk is too high and the profit too low. When activists conducted this on a small scale in rural India and Bangladesh, as a form of social activism, with no profit margin and a very long time-line for recipients to pay the debt back, it worked in some small but significant ways (Hashemi et al. 2004). The NGO they founded, the Grameen Bank, offered a kind of semi-civic self-help that was supposed to "empower women," and "build social capital" – "social capital" being the phrase that people like Putnam use to describe the dense network of ties that are supposed to lead to economic development, according to the theory. Micro-credit almost never helped the poorest of the poor, but only those poor people who were ambitious enough to think of becoming small entrepreneurs (Elyachar 2005). For this purpose, micro-credit had been helpful. But when other banks got involved, the monetary bottom line reasserted itself once again. These banks say that they are promoting sustainable development, but they usually mean "sustainable" in terms of the market. In other words, they usually measure "success" in financial terms, not in terms of how well it helps the poor (Haase 2012). It is not impossible to retain the dual missions, especially, according to one case study, if the organization focuses on its very long-term health as an organization, rather than on quick results (Battilana and Dorado 2010: 14–27), but often, the mission of helping the poor recedes while the money-making mission advances. In other words, when the small micro-finance program went big and started taking the mission of market sustainability seriously, it often lost its mission of helping the poor.

For these NGOs, the goal is to fund self-sustaining enterprises. The idea smuggled in, inside the idea of "sustainable," is that if it is good, it can make money or that people can help each other for free. Sometimes, impoverished people learn about self-improvement without getting access to the material means to do it, such as money for nutritious food and health care. Thick projectspeak makes it hard to know whether or not such was the case in a small South Carolina town that had

> a community visioning and strategic planning process ... involving three hundred citizens on various committees ... asset mapping [the phrase "asset mapping" comes from Asset Based Community Development, which is based on the idea that all communities have "assets," even ones that do not have money as one of their assets, and since God has given us all assets, we can all be equal through them] ... neighborhood information networks to reach out to pregnant women not receiving proper prenatal care. (Sirianni and Friedland 2001: 171)

or in a nearby small town that held

> seven community forums ... on issues such as education, economic development, intergroup relations, and healthy lifestyles ... a well-baby fair, and a ... training program on diabetes. (Ibid.)

"Community visioning," "strategic planning process," "asset mapping," "community forums," "training program:" these are some hints that a great deal of empowerment talk is in play. From these phrases, it is hard to know what participants actually did. Clearly, pamphlets with information were circulated, and indeed, if a person has enough money to buy healthful food or enough time to grow it, then such information could be a lifesaver. Making ordinary citizens responsible for their own health can help them "make healthy choices." But if a person is pregnant or has diabetes, information would not be enough. At one such "health fair" in Los Angeles, I obtained a great deal of information, including a poster listing "One Hundred Ways to Praise Your Child" from the Los Angeles Child Guidance Clinic. It is nice to praise one's child, but it made me think that they were being offered praise when what they needed was health care, food, places to get clean, fresh air and exercise, and child care.

When women in a prison that aimed to empower prisoners were educated about nutrition, no mention of cost or access was made, and then the women were reprimanded for laughing at the expensive suggestions for dietary changes (Haney 2010). In the USA, the comparison is between advice-giving versus no health care, so in this comparison, giving out information looks like a step ahead. But in, for example, Canada, the contrast is between getting advice and well-meaning volunteers, on the one hand, versus getting nationally funded health care, on the other hand. When the province of Ontario tried to decentralize its health care system by sharing responsibilities with civic associations, the result, according to two scholars (Jensen and Phillips 2000) was that everyone spent more time writing grants and scrambling for money than ever before, more civic associations were part of a giant semi-government octopus with tentacles holding onto what had once been independent civic associations, and health care did not improve.

A famous case that seems, on the face of it, to illustrate the potential of a little seed money plus a little voluntarism to add up to a fully self-sustaining organization is Homeboys Industries. A priest got former gang members in an impoverished East Los Angeles neighborhood to learn to bake and to sell their muffins, bread, cupcakes, and croissants. The program seemed to show clear as day that if only ghetto people got the entrepreneurial spirit and a small financial jumpstart, they would spring out of poverty. The organization added on a gardening business, silk-screening company, tattoo-removal, day care, and other businesses. By 2010, the NGO generated about $3.5 million a year, according to its founder (Zavis 2010). But when donations started drying up after the financial crash of 2008, it became clear that the Homeboys Industries depended on donations. It still needed another seven million dollars a year from donors to continue to operate. Various government and private donors kicked in, to make this organization continue its valuable work. It was not a profit-making enterprise. It was not a good poster child for self-help – unless, that is, we include as a "self-help" the fact that Homeboys Industries successfully marketed its worthiness, attracting donors to give money to it instead of to another potentially worthy cause.

One solution to the puzzle of matching all the criss-crossed missions is to drop the myth of "self-help," and instead, to create an organization in which volunteers learn a great deal, but which does not become self-sustaining in the market. Homeboys Industries illustrates this solution. Another, more typical, solution is to drop the mission of "helping the needy" – or at least avoid helping the most needy and focus instead on the people who might already be on their way up.

If an organization turns away the clients who are the most expensive to serve, the result is called "cherry-picking," "skimming the cream," or "picking the lowest hanging fruit." A homeless shelter that turns away people who are mentally ill or have drinking problems, for example, will be easier and cheaper to maintain than one that serves all people (Smith and Lipsky 1995). A private school that turns away disabled pupils will serve more children cheaply than one that accepts children who need special, potentially expensive accommodations. The monetary root of the temptation to "cherry pick" is obvious: the organization will quickly and easily show to donors that it gets more for its money. Unlike governments, NGOs' funding is usually temporary and short term. Even when funding comes from the government, it comes in the form of competitive grants, and each year or half year, the NGOs have to compete with one another all over again. Often, any single program has to appeal to many diverse financial sponsors, each with its own criteria of a good performance. All of this adds up to immense pressure to get quick results that can be easily displayed to distant, hurried, fickle audiences.

In sum, when these programs try to empower participants themselves, as a route out of poverty, they can easily end up "blaming the victim" (Ryan 1976). Or they can end up helping the people who already are in a good position to help themselves, at the expense of the more downtrodden. These are not insurmountable risks, but tendencies that these short-term projects share.

Tension 2: Appreciation for unique people and unique cultures versus quick transparency

Can an empowerment program respect the local people's intimate grassroots knowledge of their local problems, wishes, and desires and *also, simultaneously,* transparently justify expenditures, so distant funders can quickly understand and agree with the ways their money is being used?

When scholars talk about this dilemma, they usually talk about conscious disagreements, so we can start there: Local people and global donors might not agree about what is good. The local folk might say something like this: "if your aid agency claims that it wants to respect local traditions, then you should fund our local, traditionally rooted civic associations even if you consider them to be sexist!" In some societies, for example, It seems obvious that we should prevent harmful practices – terrible rites of passage that young people undergo when they reach puberty, or the traditional Inuit hunting for baby seals, for example – until we realize that it is part of the local culture's time-bound tradition, or at least some powerful local people think it is.

For example, your NGO might claim that you respect local traditions, but you might actively try to *destroy* the local traditions that you consider barbarically violent. *Sometimes*, it works. In the early 1900s, the wife of a British missionary in China started Mrs Little's Natural Foot Society. She was on a crusade against foot-binding. Foot-binding involved breaking girls' foot bones so that they could be shaped into tiny pods that were hard to walk on, but that men of the era found irresistibly attractive. It was hard for a woman with normal feet to find a husband. Mrs Little's campaign worked partly because local elites said that the old tradition of foot-binding violated an even older aspect of Chinese tradition:

honoring one's parents. The natural foot is a gift from one's parents, and besides, "a natural footed woman could buy medicine for a sick parent in less time than it took for a foot-bounded woman." The elites also wanted China to modernize, and they aligned themselves against foot-binding because they thought it made China look ridiculous on the world stage. In 1890, nearly 99 percent of women in one rural area near Beijing had their feet bound; by 1919, no new feet got bound (Keck and Sikkink 1998; Appiah 2010).

Mrs Little's success with large feet looks like a perfect illustration of the power of transnational activism, when it has human rights – freedom from unnecessary pain, in this case – on its side. But then, consider a contrasting case. When similar foreigners tried to end female genital cutting in Kenya, Somalia, and Senegal, it failed. This is a rite of passage for girls, which involves cutting off parts of their labia or clitoris. It can lead to loss of sexual pleasure, pain with intercourse, infection, menstrual problems, or even death. Westerners have been mounting campaigns against it since the 1920s, and none have succeeded the way the free-foot campaigns did in China.

Why not? They are similar, in many ways. Like foot-binding, genital cutting was considered normal and traditional. Like Chinese women with natural feet in the 1890s, Kenyan women with natural genitals were often rejected by potential mates. Like having one's foot bound, genital mutilation was considered a rite of passage – part of what one did to become a woman, and something that many young women actively *wanted* (kind of like a more extreme version of wearing uncomfortably high heels or having plastic surgery to reduce or enlarge body parts, in some "modern" societies today). Why did one succeed and the other fail? Scholars have explained it by observing that the Chinese campaigns included encouraging local people to form civic *associations*, in which parents would vow not to bind their girls' feet and, equally importantly, to encourage their sons to marry girls with unbound feet. The African campaigns included no such associations. Instead, to make change happen the foreigners in Africa tried to outlaw genital cutting. It was a top-down imposition from the foreign colonizers. The colonial rulers' orders from on high amplified mounting anti-colonial sentiment in the region.

This is the problem with treating the local culture as a frozen, unchanging thing: it is not. As the China case showed, deciding what to count as "our culture" is an ongoing argument; while some Chinese people in the late 1800s considered foot-binding to be deeply part of the culture, others could point out that being able to help one's parents – by running to find help for them if necessary – was also part of Chinese culture. In both continents, people began to see themselves as actors on the world stage; appealing to people's desire not to want to appear backward was part of what helped the Chinese campaign win. In the African cases, the culture became increasingly opposed to colonization, in response to brutal colonial efforts. Activists have to recognize that they cannot come in from afar and freeze people's culture at one moment in the past, according to one subgroup's version of that culture. Cultures do not stand still. People argue about what their culture is. And sometimes, this is a good thing, but it does not coincide with NGOs constant effort to identify and affirm local people's culture.

These cases show conscious disagreements between donors and recipients. But there is another aspect to the tension between the quest to respect local cultures and the need to convince distant hurried funders, which is less conscious and therefore harder to fix. When agencies fund civic associations, they *have* to make judgments about what is "good." NGOs have to know what they are funding. They *have to* have guidelines. The problem is that whether the project is to bring aid from Denmark to Albania or from Beverly Hills to nearby LA ghettos, the guidelines originate in the provider's conditions (nation, or class, or lifestyle, or locale), and often do not fit the receiver's conditions (Bob 2004, 2005). Many perfectly worthy projects do not easily measure up in ways that distant, hurried audiences will easily recognize.

Recognizing this tension helps explain why, for example, some desperate situations abroad become *causes célèbres*, and not others. The movements that gain international appeal are those that figure out how to match what donors want. The Ogoni people of the Nigerian Delta, for example, live in an area that has oil, and Royal Dutch Shell has been extracting their oil, destroying the environment that the Ogoni needed for survival. This incited an international outcry about Shell's exploitation of their labor and destruction of their environment. The leader of the Ogoni people has a degree from Oxford and is well-connected with international elites. "By contrast, other Niger Delta 'oil minorities' have not had the Ogonis' wealthy, knowledgeable, and well-connected leaders." The Ogoni people managed to figure out how to market their problem to distant funders. Staff of international NGOs– Greenpeace International and Friends of the Earth International – explained to sociologist Clifford Bob that the Ogoni's first efforts at marketing failed, because they "appeared deeply enmeshed in murky and difficult issues of Nigerian politics, issues that did not match the NGOs' environmental agendas" (Bob 2002: 142). So, the local people who can "frame" their problem in a way that faraway people can understand quickly win.

On the face of it, this does not seem so terrible. So what if donors only help some people? At least they have helped somebody. But there are two huge problems with this marketing: first, when the local organization has to shape its work to appeal to faraway donors, there is a danger that the organizers will focus their attention abroad and lose touch with their local base. The organization might start working on projects that faraway donors like, at the expense of working on projects that the local people need (Bob 2005). Worse, the donations could easily set one group ahead of another. The ethnic groups that are good at marketing their suffering could go far ahead of the others, and inequalities could develop that were not there before. Becoming so much stronger than their neighbors, the good marketers could exploit their neighbors. Another possible consequence of this marketing is that the more easily marketable solution can undermine a less marketable solution. Some solutions are hard to describe in ways that distant, hurried, multiple funders can easily understand. When international human rights groups campaign against sex trafficking, they might not know what alternatives the women face. Some of the women say that the alternatives are worse. It is easy to market outrage against sex trafficking, and force the sex workers to go back to their home countries. It is harder to market outrage over the homegrown abuse and hunger that the women suffer when they are sent home (Parreñas 2011). Similarly, many international human rights NGOs campaign against the use of child soldiers in Burma. This sounds like an obviously good cause, but many *other* human rights NGOs rely on these child soldiers to escort them into conflict-ridden zones, where these NGOs provide much-needed aid. There is also a question regarding what alternatives some of these children have at the moment. Without giving them a realistic alternative, the NGOs could be putting the children in the position of choosing between fighting in battle versus dying at home (Dale 2010). This is like the choice that Jane Addams confronted, when she saw families having to choose between sending their children to work versus going homeless: the whole situation is wrong. Like the Nigerian case, the situation is "murky" and answers are not clear cut.

The clash between real-life murkiness and donors' need for speed and clarity sharpens when confronted by a relatively recent invention: organizations that monitor charities, such as Charity Navigator, measure the financial health of an organization in ways that emphasize the charity's efficient, effective use of money. This sounds undeniably good, until one ponders what could have improved the outcomes in any of the above tales. What if more research into the everyday conditions of life in Albania or Burma would have helped NGOs invest more wisely? Research is expensive, and if an NGO is evaluated by its financial health, then one that does the job more quickly and inexpensively, with less overhead, would win more stars.

There are other, wrenching tragic dangers in trying to market a culture to faraway donors. There are often subtle difficulties in deciding *what to count* as local and authentic. A civic association that wins foreign donors' dollars has to look "authentic," which often means that it has to *look like* it is promoting the image of local culture that the distant funders have. NGO funders in Thailand, for example, "build civil society" by helping local people market their truly "authentic" handmade, folkloric wooden items abroad (Wherry 2012). When the people in Berlin, Tokyo, New York, and

Paris buy those handmade objects, those local folks in Thailand can use their new income to buy flat screen televisions, consume more, and develop more of a taste for foreign consumer goods, thus getting tightly yoked to the global economy. This could undermine whatever local culture and economy they may have managed to preserve thus far. Now, they can surf the web . . . but only after work hours, when they are not busy being folklorically authentic. Making their culture into a saleable item can undermine the local folks' feeling that the culture is really theirs. Furthermore, the process can help some people leap far ahead of their neighbors. Those who can package their culture in palatable ways for distant foreigners become wealthy, while others lag behind. When some people jump far ahead, it can lure everyone into the competitive quest to be the first among equals. Another dilemma is that the newly richer can easily turn their new-found wealth into power, and use it to exploit their neighbors.

In sum, empowerment projects' mission of honoring unique persons and places often come into conflict with the programs' need for quick, easy to decipher documentation for hurried, distant funders. Some organizations give elaborate documentation that takes details and variations into account, and that are difficult to decipher. It takes time, and often requires some expertise to decipher data like this. But remember: one key characteristic of these programs is that they have short-term funding, and non-expert donors who might change their minds if the program is too hard to grasp quickly.

Tension 3: Appreciation for unique people and cultures versus catalyzing personal transformation versus transparency for distant, hurried donors

Participating in these civic groups is supposed to produce unique, personal intimacy between members. It is also supposed to be personally transformative. It has to happen quickly enough to explain to funders in time for the next funding cycle, and in ways that distant others could easily grasp without spending a lot of time doing research about them.

Empowerment projects try to preserve unique cultures. They also try to change the participants, to touch their souls, to inspire and transform the participants in a deep way. This presents a tension: preserve or change? At a workshop for adult volunteers in Snowy Prairie, a librarian was teaching potential adult volunteers about "multicultural literature." A puzzled adult volunteer asks how you can tell what counts as multicultural.

> The librarian answers, "Just make sure that once you find a book that it's ok. Just because it has images of multicultural kids doesn't mean it's a good book. Some of us might remember Little Black Sambo from our own childhood: today, if we looked at it, we would see that Little Black Sambo is not giving kids a good image of themselves."
>
> Another audience member asks same question, and the librarian responds, "You have to go with your gut feelings. If you're reading along and it makes you uncomfortable, go with your gut. You know the kids and what they like. Go with your gut." (Eliasoph 2011: 195)

These volunteers might have considered Little Black Sambo to be part of their culture, and they might have cherished the memory of sitting on Grandpa's knee reading it. NGOs are not supposed to take sides, so the librarian could only say, "Go with your gut," as if the gut would always go the right way. If guts always went the right way, why did anyone *ever* like Little Black Sambo, then?

Similarly, in a support group for parents of lesbians and gays, participants are supposed to look inside themselves to find how they really feel about their children. There, deep inside, they are expected to locate that sweet spot of acceptance and openness. If they do not, but instead, find homophobia, dismay, or shock at their gay son or lesbian daughter, the workshop leaders tell them that they have not gone deep enough; they have not found their "real self" (Psihopaidas 2012). Their really real self, according to this approach, is not ambivalent, not mixed, but pure and certain. This is one way of smoothing out the tension between the missions of "appreciating unique individuals and cultures" versus "catalyzing personal transformation;" to proceed as if the personal transformation had already unequivocally taken place.

Another dilemma comes from this tangle of missions that includes appreciating unique selves while also pushing volunteers to have – and display – personal transformation in ways that everyone can appreciate quickly and without too much personal disturbance. While empowerment projects are supposed to appreciate unique individuals, they are also supposed to transform them by bringing about deeply emotional encounters between *diverse* people. They are supposed to "celebrate diversity," as they often put it, but the diversity has to be easy to see quickly, for those distant, hurried, varied potential grant-givers and potential volunteers. In Snowy Prairie, this usually meant making sure that non-white youths appeared in public events – even though organizers knew that many white youth had problems. Their problems – abuse, neglect, mental or physical illness, addiction – were too hard to make public.

Personal transformation rarely is this rapid, so empowerment projects have to find a way to give participants and viewers an impression of transformation without necessarily waiting till it happens. One approach is to project it, as if to say that there is a possibility that it will happen if you stayed in the project long enough (which you probably won't). For example, meetings in empowerment projects often start with "ice-breakers:" group games intended to help participants get to know one another. The problem in Snowy Prairie was that people never said anything unique or personal about themselves. One ice-breaker, for example, was a circle game, in which one person got in the middle and said, "I'm on a train, and I'm taking anyone who . . ." and they filled in the blank: wears jeans, like soccer, for example. Everyone who shared that quality had to run to the middle and find a place across the circle. The last one in the middle was "it," and the game began again. Participants said things like "I'm taking anyone who likes pizza, wears jeans, has straight hair," and never said things like "has a father in prison, has a serious digestive problem, or is not Christian."

This became a problem when participants were supposed to share their personal, emotionally intense stories with one another. If a person's story was actually unique, it took too long to share.

The result was often that people had to expose an "intimate" self that was standardized and sanitized – unique, but not too unique, troubled, or out of control. In theory, appreciating diversity meant appreciating each unique individual, but actually, it meant appreciating people as members of visible categories – visible so the donors could see diversity instantly, without examining statistical tables or health records. If anyone had problems that were really not typical for the others in the room, the problem was usually too embarrassing to be discussed in public, or took too long to explain.

Another puzzle arises with merging this quest for emotionally rewarding experiences with empowerment projects' other missions. Earlier, we saw that organizations that pick the easiest to solve cases can be accused of "cherry-picking." But as *Making Volunteers* shows, volunteers' quest for inspiring experiences provides an additional force steering organizations toward cherry-picking. Adult volunteers came to help in the after-school homework programs, wanting a rewarding experience, but have only one or two hours a week to spare. At one of the programs, they would literally run to the table of girls who were eager to do their homework, sometimes actually pushing each other out of the way to get there, to make sure that they – the volunteers – got an emotionally rewarding experience this afternoon. One gloomy boy with greasy hair and a dirty windbreaker sat alone for weeks at a time. No volunteer offered him help. It looked like it would not be emotionally rewarding for the *volunteer*.

Tension 4: Helping the needy versus hands-on, non "expert"-based appreciation of unique people: the temptation to avoid politics

Empowerment projects have to draw on local folks' non-expert wisdom to help the needy, rather than relying on distant experts like the ones who created disasters like Pruitt-Igoe. Sometimes, however, paid professionals or semi-professionals are more in touch with local, unique people and customs than volunteers are.

On first glance, it may appear as if the only reason that an NGO would avoid hiring expert help is that it is expensive. Another, related reason is one we have already described: since NGOs' funding is usually temporary and comes from multiple, hurried sources, it is better not to have to explain experts' complicated decision-making processes to donors who will not have the time to research the complex decision-making. It is tempting to pick the lowest hanging fruit – the problems that do not require experts to solve – and tout the organization's easy victories. Saving money is, indeed, an important reason for avoiding experts.

But there are other reasons that empowerment projects try to avoid experts. One is that the presence of unpaid volunteers symbolizes, in funders' eyes, that a program enjoys local grassroots support, and is not just a creation of distant abstract experts. In Snowy Prairie, for example, paid organizers had to welcome these volunteers with open arms – even if the volunteers were harmful. Adult volunteers come to help their after-school program, promising to become like "beloved aunties" to them, but they have only two hours a week for three months to spare for the purpose. The adult volunteers do not know enough about each child to help with homework. The young people get contradictory advice on how to complete any given homework assignment. On some long-term homework assignments – a history essay, for example – program participants got different suggestions for how to organize it each day, for two weeks. Sometimes, the advice given one hour contradicted the advice given the next hour, if, for example, one volunteer left mid afternoon and another came to take his or her place. The adult volunteers wanted a rewarding experience, and so if the child did not want to do homework, the adult would find another way to make the experience rewarding: to bond by having a snowball fight in the street at dusk for example. Then the paid organizer had to come discipline the children and the adult volunteers as well. If the volunteer succeeded and opened up, and then the volunteer left after a couple of months, as many in Snowy Prairie did, a child who was already fragile could easily learn from this that opening up emotionally is a big mistake (Rhodes and Grossman 2002).

Sometimes, it would have been easier and more effective if the paid staff person had just directly helped the client. Certain paid organizers in Snowy Prairie helped the kids do their homework and maintained a comfortable, "family-like" atmosphere more easily after the adult volunteers went home. The adult volunteers' presence usually undermined the intimacy that long-term, experienced paid organizers sometimes manage to establish.

Another reason that empowerment projects try to avoid experts is that experts can be boring. It might be more appealing to more numbers of people to give emotionally powerful stories instead of dry analyses. This is a dilemma not just for empowerment projects, but also for NGOs that are not empowerment projects that mainly want to convince a specialized audience to change a policy. Human Rights Watch, for example, is an organization that publicizes human rights violations around the world. It has to mount fairly dry, detailed, legal arguments, and many layers of statistics, to convince international human rights lawyers. In the process, HRW often convinces the public, but its main audience is in high courts. However, to document their claims, researchers have to go to the places where the violations are occurring, and it is a harrowing experience. It is hard for these researchers and lawyers to keep themselves from showing their feelings when they testify in court. So there is still a tension between caring feelings and emotions, versus arguments that are dry and hard to follow, about law and justice. But HRW's answer is different from an empowerment project's typical answer. The international rights lawyers assume that they have to *hide* their emotions when they are presenting their legal cases. Yet, to their other audience – the general public – HRW has to present personal stories, usually using one person's emotionally wrenching tale to stand in for thousands of others (Gray 2012). Bringing the two into harmony is difficult. These lawyers are, after all, in it for emotional, caring, moral reasons, not because they worship the letter of the law itself. For the purpose of gathering donations from the general public, personal, emotional story-telling works better than legal arguments. But these kinds of arguments discredit the researchers when they are speaking to lawyers, who demand cool-headed logic.

As noted earlier, time-consuming investigations are not usually on the agenda for volunteers and donors in empowerment projects. This is another way that an organization like HRW differs from an empowerment project. Because empowerment projects are always pressed for time, it is easier for NGOs to conduct volunteer-style projects than to dig out problems' roots. For example, international NGOs often promise to give individual donors a feeling of hands-on contact with the recipients of their aid. This mission often comes at the expense of serious help for the needy. The Heifer Foundation is one such international NGO. This international Christian Aid organization's glossy brochure appeals to individual donors, asking them to buy animals for poor families in impoverished countries. A water buffalo might suit a Filipino family, for example:

> A water buffalo can lead a hungry family out of poverty and give them a chance for a bright future filled with hope and free from hunger . . . Water buffalo haul heavy loads to the market, where the sale of extra produce brings in vital income for clothing, medicine and school. By renting their buffalo to neighbors, Heifer partner families can earn money for home improvements. And one day, those same neighbors might receive a water buffalo of their own as recipients pass on the gifts of animals and training.
> From https://secure1.heifer.org/gift-catalog/water-buffalo.html/?msou rce=kwgb31&gclid=CL7nxMjJqK4CFQZchwod3RPxDQ (retrieved February 10, 2012)

Here we see the idea we encountered earlier: changing the world, one x at a time. It is a colorful, easy to grasp, seemingly quick and simple solution to a complex problem.

Again, how could it possibly be harmful to help someone? As will be documented in chapter 5, inequality is just as harmful to people's health as raw poverty, down to a surprisingly low point of poverty. Imagine what happens: two families are struggling side-by-side in poverty. Along comes this gift water buffalo, but only to Family A, who now is the renter to Family B. The whole power balance in the village is upset. What if Family A buys other families' land? Or imagine that Family A gets a big TV and charges rent for Family B to come to watch. Unless the Heifer Foundation gives every family in the village a heifer at once, it is easy to imagine that a few families will use their new wealth to gain power to lord it over the village. So why doesn't the Heifer Foundation wait and give the whole village a lot of water buffaloes at once? Perhaps it is because donors want to help one individual right now, not wait till there is enough money to help a whole village. Individual donors want to know how much their specific donation has quickly made a difference to an individual family's life!

When we read in their catalogue that a donation of ten chickens or three rabbits might make the difference between life and death in a family, we are not encouraged to ask why a few chickens would not be a matter of life and death for one of us, or for one of the dozen or so billionaires who have seized control of the world's wealth. This would involve us in messy and hard-to-follow arguments. It would take too much time and invoke political controversy. So even if addressing this big issue could potentially provide enough eggs and rabbit meat for millions of people at once, and worse, even if *not* addressing it could lead to harm, the question is too abstract, big, and complicated in the eyes of most members of the donor-public.

The result can often be that empowerment projects ask people to plug a small hole in the dam when the entire dam is crumbling. Here is another example: at the same time that Habitat for Humanity is enlisting perky volunteers to build houses, banks that have foreclosed on houses have been finding it cheaper to tear the whole house down in some cities, than to make small repairs and resell them (Tyler 2012). What if Habitat for Humanity volunteers are building homes more slowly than bankers are tearing them down? What if more people would get homes if Habitat for Humanity volunteers studied and publicized what they learned about the banking disaster, so that fewer homes would get torn down?

Plugging a small hole seems relatively harmless; after all, the presence of the humanitarian aid organization did not *cause* the homeless person to be homeless. Did it? Well, sometimes, the humanitarian NGO can actually cause harm. We saw some hints of this earlier in this chapter, with sex trafficking, for example, when humanitarian NGOs' work results in the sex worker's being sent home to conditions that are often far more dangerous than ones from which the NGO rescued her. The NGOs want to avoid tackling the bigger problem of dangerous and subhuman labor conditions worldwide, by focusing only on one specific type of exploited labor: sex work. But they cannot solve the seemingly smaller problem without engaging the bigger one (Parreñas 2011). Another illustration of this problem comes from humanitarian relief efforts in Africa, for example, that help displaced persons with food, shelter, and medical care. What could possibly go wrong with that, one might wonder? In situations of civil war, fighters come to the refugee camps to refuel with food and to get medical treatment, so that they can rush back into the fight (Cook 2011). Humanitarian NGOs working in such situations estimate that a full half of their food supplies disappear – most of it, presumably, into the combatants' camps, often fueling both sides of an explosive fight at once. On the other hand, when humanitarian aid projects *do* try to turn away combatants, the result can also be disastrous, if most of the population is somehow connected to the conflict. It can lead to denying vital care to people who have been caught in the middle. An organization may well decide to give aid to everyone who comes, even combatants, because it is universally the humanitarian thing to do, but otherwise, an organization would have to spend a great deal of money and time figuring out how to screen people. Then, the organization would have to educate donors who might lose patience.

However hard NGOs try to avoid taking a side and to steer completely clear of politics, it is impressively difficult for another reason. Starting with disasters like the Galveston Hurricane of 1901, the Red Cross had a hard time deciding whom to count as a "a suffering victim of a natural disaster" (someone they would serve) versus a person who is simply suffering from a poor economy or someone who is just suffering from being poor (people they would not serve) (Potts 2012). It has been hard for disaster relief organizations to make sure that they were not feeding people who had been homeless or hungry *before* the disaster. Such people would not be considered victims of the disaster. Of course, each organization has to carve out a finite population to serve, but this is the problem that political activists confront head-on; when they pull out one thread of the scarf, the whole thing starts to unravel. Everything is connected.

Some scholars argue that when experts get involved, organizers stop asking big political questions. Is it true? A case they use to make this point is the evolution of battered women's shelters in the USA (Smith and Lipsky 1995). In the 1970s, unpaid feminist activists started to open up shelters that gave domestic violence victims a temporary place to stay. The activists attributed domestic violence to overarching gender inequality. They saw the whole system as connected: if, as noted in chapter 2, marital rape was a legal impossibility before the 1980s (because the wife was considered the husband's property), then the feminist founders of the original battered women's shelters aimed for an overarching radical change in the definition of "man," "woman," and "marriage." They first wanted stable state funding. After all, protection from violence is clearly in the government's scope. But these early feminists saw that as only the first, most basic step in a larger war against gender norms. They won the battle, but some say they lost the war. Did they? Now, these shelters are usually NGOs that get government funding. They hire professional social workers, which means that unpaid volunteers have less decision-making power. And now that money is important, a quick turn-around time of the funding cycle tends to make an organization become less politically confrontational (Smith and Lipsky 1995: 83–5).

So are these NGOs less politically engaged because they are more professional? As Jane Addams and the participants in the radical social work movement have said and shown over the past century, it is just as likely that the opposite is true (Wagner 1989; Schudson 2006). Indeed, part of what expertise might mean is knowledge about how to get ordinary people involved in decision-making ways that genuinely will help them. Organizations that get government funding usually have to have experts with specialized degrees – in law, medicine, nursing, accounting, for example – and these organizations are no less politically active than those that do not get funding (Chaves et al. 2004). Professionals, especially professional social workers, may have enough experience, and enough of the big picture, to "connect the dots." They may have entered their profession with big ideas about political transformation in the first place, and now, twenty years later, the same ideas inspire them (Sirianni and Friedland 2001). Further, donors might expect professionals to investigate each case in a more complex way than volunteers could, which takes time. The professionals might be able to convince donors and volunteers alike that the demand for rapid, measurable results is unrealistic, if the goal is deep political change. Deep transformation is usually slow.

It should be noted, again, that many NGOs are NOT empowerment projects, but are "advocacy" organizations like Human Rights Watch that just aim to promote a policy, publicize an issue, convince people to take one political position over another. These projects do not have the same dilemmas as empowerment projects, or when they do, they usually come down on different sides of them. They tend to carry on their debates among experts and lay-experts. For example, an organization that tries to educate people about genetic engineering, Genetics and Society, does not try to empower "the average citizen," but mainly speaks to people who have some connection to genetics, such as scientists, doctors, people involved in reproductive rights, and disability rights activists. Human Rights Watch, as noted, mainly speaks to lawyers and experts in high courts. It is not trying to empower anyone, but relies on experts, and works with a familiar stable full of regulators, lawyers, politicians, and other specialists. Empowerment projects, in contrast, have a vague constituency that they hope, in part, to create through "empowerment:" this mythical constituency is what the empowerment project personnel call "the public."

Expert, technological advice, and political avoidance

Some international aid projects are not quite empowerment projects, either. They do not claim to shun expertise and do not expect to empower the volunteers. When they help faraway people who want something very specific – a water works for their region, for example – they are some of the most effective international NGOs (Edwards 2009). Engineers Without Borders, Doctors Without Borders, Globe Med, Global Architecture Brigades, and Habitat for Humanity are some of the organizations that draw on volunteers' professional expertise or energy to address problems that are often occurring far from the volunteer's daily life. Some of these organizations' leaders have a broad political vision about redistributing wealth worldwide, and others don't, but they all appeal to funders and volunteers with a story that is much more circumscribed and expert-oriented than an empowerment project would be.

With Engineers Without Borders, for example, waves of volunteers have gone from the USA to Guatemala to build one water system, in one small region, over the course of three years. This kind of project fulfills some of the "empowering" missions for the volunteers: it gives volunteers a chance to do something that might transform them personally, and also gives them a good line on a CV, for future employment. But more broadly, projects like Engineers Without Borders have to leave aside several of empowerment projects' other crisscrossed missions: The volunteers cannot expect quick and deep inspiration. Their work is mostly not hands-on, up-close and personal; the engineers' main work happens in their home base, for example. These volunteers have to trust their project leaders to have studied the locale, to avoid finding themselves in the middle of a conflict, and possibly inadvertently fueling it. The volunteers do not necessarily have to learn about local politics themselves to be helpful engineers, but if they do not, then they miss many of the lessons in citizenship that Tocqueville hoped volunteers would learn. The engineers will not learn how to gain power, the way Tocqueville thought volunteers might learn. Gaining power for themselves is not the engineers' goal. It would be a travesty if the engineers wanted a say in political decisions regarding a road-building project, for example, and judged from afar which faction in the village deserved the road more. Instead, they temporarily give themselves over to the local people, putting themselves wholly in their service, to help them get something they need.

In other words, if the main goal is helping the needy, this might be more effective than trying to empower the volunteer and make him or her appreciate unique people and cultures. More generally, this solution is to hand the volunteers a very limited, specific task: read this book with this first grader, then that book with that one; figure out a specific engineering component of this hydraulic system in this hillside in Guatemala; build that house for that one family. The result may very well be helpful.

On the other hand, even here, in this seemingly neutral, apolitical project, there is a long history of harms done. In the 1970s, the Green Revolution's promise was that a technological solution – the invention of super-productive, patented seeds that thrived only with massive inputs of fertilizer and pesticide – could solve the problem of world hunger without having to address the political problem of world inequality. One problem, as discussed in chapter 3, is that faraway experts *can* create problems; the petrochemical inputs seemed like a good idea from faraway experts' perspective, but up close, it started to become clear that they had a high cost to the soil and water, and fertility has declined back to a level even lower than where it started, in some places (Cullather 2010). Now, as a response, a movement for "appropriate technology" aims to take local ecological and social conditions into account rather than assuming that the most high-tech solution is the best. A second problem with this technological solution has been, according to several studies (Cullather 2010; Lappé et al. 1998; George 1986), that hunger exists mainly wherever only a few landowners control the land. In places in which land is held more equitably, there is not as much hunger, and the high-tech seeds have not fixed the more basic problem. The inputs are expensive, so only well-to-do farmers can afford them – and in this way, local inequality often increases when the new technologies arrive. Many of the seeds are non-reproducing and patented by big corporation that reap huge profits every time farmers have to plant a new season's crop – and in this way, global inequality increases. The root of the hunger problem, according to these studies, is not a lack of food but a lack of political will to distribute land to the poor. To predict and thereby prevent this disaster, supporters would have needed a political analysis, and activism, not just a technology; even when a problem looks purely technical, there is often a political problem underneath. People cannot solve this problem without confronting its political root.

Other seemingly technical issues turn out to work in a similar way, as mainly political problems rather than merely technical ones: as a student of mine pointed out, when she was switching from an engineering major to a social science major, the problem is often a lack of "political will," not a lack of high-tech innovation. Her example was this: our campus eateries use "compostable" cups, plates, and utensils for take-out foods: good technology. However, the cups and utensils end up in the same landfill as the rest of the garbage, where they do not compost, even though technologically, they could compost, if they were placed in dirt and exposed to sunlight. Someone would have to set up a special set of garbage pick-ups to make it work, and that would require more than just buying different cups. Buying different cups is like a "changing the world one x at a time" solution.

Social service NGOs and political engagement of a highly specific nature

One subset of empowerment projects are those that are engaged in providing direct social services – for free or low-cost day care, for example. They sometimes do stir up political controversy, but in a way that is quite particular to this specific sort of organization. To get government funding, leaders of some community-based organizations rally members to protest and write letters to politicians demanding more funding. In exchange, the members get more services (Marwell 2004). More broadly, minority-based activist groups have, over the past thirty years, often also become engaged in providing social services. The Urban League, for example, is an organization that aims to work on behalf of African Americans. When they also started providing services, like after-school care, some researchers argue that they did not lose their political edge. They could do both: social service and activism (Minkoff 2002).

Is this just self-interested action aimed at getting more for one's own organization, or is it activism aimed at a broader good? It depends on how participants talk about the issues. The great promise of civic associations is that they can sometimes teach people how to care about the greater good, so that participants will not just cry "not in my backyard," but "not in anyone's backyard." Seeing oppressed people operate in their own self-interest makes us cheer. But what if we, the observers, did not agree that those people were oppressed? White racists feel oppressed, too (Blee 2003), so if the white Aryan Nation, for example, claims that white people are an oppressed group, would we cheer when they press for their "rights?" The question would be how they, or any activists, transform their own wants into issues of justice (Pitkin 1980). Does their political activism include a concern for other people across town whose plight might be worse than theirs?

Some empowerment projects engage in political activism. But as described earlier, there is tremendous pressure to convey easy messages to distant hurried funders and thus, to avoid complicated political controversies that might take too long to explain. They need simple solutions to complex problems. Delving into the complexities of Nigerian politics in the Ogoni case turned off funders (Bob 2005). Talking politics might turn off volunteers who want to care about people without caring about politics (Eliasoph 1998). There are some remarkable exceptions to this, which we will describe in the final chapter.

The Home Turf of Neo-Liberalism: Empowerment Projects

All together, these tensions that empowerment projects face tend toward echoing the tensions of "neo-liberalism." When social scientists talk about neo-liberalism, they are referring, in general, to an economic and political system that tips the Tocquevillean balance all the way over to the market and voluntary sector, and away from the government. Charity will, according to a renowned economist who has been a major proponent of this faith in the market, fill in the gaps that the market might not have reached

(Friedman and Friedman 1980). If a charity does not garner enough attention, it probably was not a good one, in this perspective. People are naturally competitive, calculating, rational actors, according to this political-economic theory. If people are "liberated" to operate as free, informed agents making choices on a free market, they will find and fund what is of value, and voluntarily support causes that they consider worthy and people whom they consider worthy. Presumably, the rest were not very valuable or worthy in the first place, and losing the competition will have the happy result of lessening their future influence, or killing them off.

The term "neo-liberal" is confusing in American English because it means almost the opposite of what we call "liberal." "Liberals," in normal American English, are the people who advocate "social citizenship," the importance of a state to make sure that rich and poor children start with equal chances. The people we call "liberals" in American English (people who are also called "Left-wing" here) might have gotten the name originally because they favored "liberating" the government from any state religion, "liberating" women from traditional inequalities, and "liberating" children from unconditional obedience to authority. But that is not the meaning of "neo-liberalism." "Neo-liberalism" is mainly about letting the market make all, or nearly all, decisions about how a society should run, on the assumption that people and organizations that cannot become "sustainable" in a competitive market do not deserve to survive, or at least do not deserve to thrive. In other words, it is nearly the opposite of what Americans normally mean by "liberal."

All the components of neo-liberalism are present in the empowerment projects described in this chapter. According to neo-liberal theory, if people had a sense of personal responsibility, they would make good choices and lift themselves out of poverty, or out of any other troubles they may have. Empowerment projects aim to make people responsible, as if a lack of personal responsibility were their only problem. The programs offer "individual choice" but do not give people the material means to make a wise choice, or even any choice at all. This neo-liberal logic extends to other, non-civic organizations, as well. In a study of a prison that operates on neo-liberal principles, prisoners are exhorted to get a high-school diploma but are not given help with homework, or any books. Then, they are reprimanded for having made poor choices when they do not end up with the diploma. The prisoners are told to improve their eating habits, with suggestions for foods that are far beyond the budgets they will have when they get home. In all of these ways, neo-liberal programs like these often "responsibilize" people by offering them "choices" without giving them the material means to make the choices (Haney 2010). And everything has to happen fast, in time for the next round of grant applications.

The illusion of free choice goes with the illusion of transparency. Neo-liberal theory would say that if high schools could compete and were not shackled by state bureaucracy, any bad school would fold after the first few hundred graduates do not get into college. Parents who do the research will know. The burden is on the individual, to make good choices – or the individual's parent, in the case of unlucky schoolchildren whose parents do not "make good choices." You have perhaps encountered this burden when trying to compare cell phone prices or evaluate different health care techniques. If every product required this many decisions, you would not get through the morning. You may remember that one of the catalysts for state regulation was *The Jungle*, a book about the food industry because it made it clear that no one can do all the research him or herself. Easy to grasp projects like the Heifer Foundation get money from individuals who do not have the time to do much research.

Some NGOs manage to resolve these tensions better than others. Those exciting exceptions will be described in the final chapter. But there is pressure, in NGOs that aim to "empower" participants, to fall prey to these systemic tensions, when civic self-help, transparency, intimacy, inspiring innovation, and helping the needy collide. Usually, one or more mission has to fall by the wayside. Usually, it is the mission of helping the needy that falls by the wayside. Why, then, do the needy so often seem to stay quiet and unrebellious? That is the topic of our next chapter.

5

*What Happens to Civic Participation
in Conditions of Vast Social
Inequality?*

This chapter examines social inequality's effect on civic participation and civic participation's effect on social inequality. Whether
the question is which associations gain power, or which individuals
gain power within an association, the answer is often fairly predictable: those who already have power from some other source,
especially money. Without some degree of social equality in income,
education, and the rest, there is a risk that "civic participation" will
just amplify pre-existing inequalities. How does this work, and
what do civic associations do to try to get past this problem?

The idea of civic associations is supposed to be that the iconic
ruddy working-class fellow in the Norman Rockwell painting
should be heard as much as anyone else. Is this a utopian goal in
a society in which money can so often buy power? Total equality
never can be reached completely, but for democracy to keep going,
perhaps people have to retain the image, as a "necessary fiction," at
least so that when they are participating in a civic group, they can
at least *try* to treat all reasonable ideas as potentially worthy, no
matter how lowly the speaker. This "necessary fiction" could also
allow people to feel outrage when they learn that a well-funded
civic association won a victory over a more grassroots, less well-
funded one, simply because the big money association outspent the
poorer one, in advertising, lobbying, and splashy public events.

Under what conditions can people cultivate this necessary
fiction? There are two questions here: first, how can the field of
civic associations be organized so that the principle that "money

talks" does not apply in the civic realm? Second, how can civic groups organize themselves internally so that everyone can participate as an equal, even lowly people who might be afraid to speak up? These are our questions for this chapter.

Is Participating in Civic Associations Like Playing on an Unlevel Playing Field?

Calling for more "participation" in grassroots associations *could* just amplify inequalities. The people who have the most economic power also have the most political and civic power. This works through various mechanisms.

The revolving door

First, there is the famous "revolving door" between corporation and political position, so an oil company's CEO is more likely than the gas station cashier to become a member of Congress. That is part of why 47 percent of Congress members are millionaires. The most spectacular recent example is in the banking industry. Banks whose executives had tight connections in government finance committees, or whose executives themselves served on Federal Reserve boards, got more of the several hundred billion dollars of federal bailout money from the government than their less "well-networked" counterparts whose executives had not moved back and forth from a bank to an agency that is supposed to oversee the banks. (Duchin and Sosyura 2012). The foxes that guarded the chicken coop won. As the Occupy movement has made clear, when the government regulators are also the heads of the banks they regulate, the synergy between political power and economic power becomes overwhelming.

Birds of a feather flocking together

The "revolving door" is really only a fraction of the story of how wealth can buy political power and nullify civic associations' promise of equal voice, though. The revolving door story is only about people's work life. Possibly even more important is the segregated nature of some civic associations. For example, at Bohemian Grove, a rustic retreat under the redwoods north of San Francisco, heads of banks and other CEOs drink and carouse together, forming tight bonds that are stronger than the kind that would be formed at work through simple calculations of self-interest, paybacks, and deal-making (Domhoff 1975 [2012]). They become friends. Paradoxically, though, these tight social bonds allow them to tighten their grip on political and economic power. Here is a voluntary association that works to amplify inequality.

Elite boarding schools encourage their students to be public spirited and to find a worthy cause into which they can pour their souls. This is considered important, not only for the cynical purpose of having something to put on a college application essay. The people who run the programs, and many of the students themselves, consider volunteer work to be crucial for building the student's character. Elites then tend to see themselves as caring stewards for the society (Khan 2011).

There is nothing inherently evil in this, if the schools make sure that students understand the larger context for their volunteer work. These schools rarely teach the students about that larger context (Khan 2011). The schools *could* show students that finding a good internship often requires connections; or that it is logistically difficult for many high-school students to get to the NGO's office for the rewarding volunteer opportunity; or that many of their poorer peers do not have time for prestigious internships, since they have to take care of younger siblings or elderly relatives, or work at a paid job after school; or that the volunteer opportunities such as "voluntourism" are often so expensive, the volunteers' budgets exceed that of the villages they aim to help. It is easy for the student and the public to treat these conditions as irrelevant. The student can drive to the volunteer opportunity but not really *see* the investment that their parents made, in the car and the gas mileage that got the student to the NGO's door (Eliasoph 2011). When prevention programs for at-risk youth have to find funds for the vehicle, it becomes a public, visible issue, and a matter for charities, to help the disadvantaged students become volunteers. A student who has more resources will be in a better position proudly to show to the world – and to him or herself – that she or he is an independent, free-willed caring steward of the world. Volunteering also gives the elite student a chance to network. When we put all this together, we arrive at a sad conclusion: while many elite students really do want to rectify social ills, and would sacrifice a great deal to do so, the painfully ironic twist is that their humble generosity can itself cause more inequality.

Control of the media

Another reason that civic life might just echo already existing inequalities is that elites can often control the terms of debate. The major news outlets have been concentrated in fewer and fewer hands each year for decades (Bagdikian 1997). Corporations and other powerful entities can make their ideas into "news;" for example, the Pentagon sends major newsrooms a really exciting video of military jets taking off, and since reporters often do not have the time or money to find critics of the jazzy new expediture, the video becomes something like an ad for exciting military expenses (Herman and Chomsky 1989).

Astroturf campaigns

There is yet another reason for the people at the top to participate more, and to get more of a bang for their buck. They can buy a civic association! With enough money, corporations and individual millionaires can subvert the equality that civic associations promise. Of course, they can buy billboard ads, magazine ads, online ads, and they can flood people's mail with flyers promoting their ideas, but this is only the most obvious tip of the iceberg.

Most of what they do is much harder to see: To make a normal activist event happen, a small handful of unpaid activists spend hundreds of unpaid hours planning and publicizing it, convincing their less passionate counterparts about the worthiness of their cause. With a few million dollars, a funder can bypass the need for unpaid activists. They can publicize civic events before any unpaid volunteers have joined, and then, when the crowd shows up, the funders can make sure that no one can trace the funding, thus making the speak-outs seem to be inspired by local, grassroots people. (O'Connor 2010).

In a book aptly titled *Toxic Sludge is Good for You: Lies, Damn Lies, and the Public Relations Industry*, John Stauber and Sheldon Rampton document several more of these techniques: Companies can pay people to come to civic events, such as when cigarette companies held a parade in New York in the early 1900s, in which women could exhibit their female liberation by smoking in public. Nearly a century later, the tobacco companies lavishly funded a fake grassroots campaign to call upon smokers to sign petitions to defend smokers' rights (Walker 2009). Companies can pay individual infiltrators to become active members of their opponents' organizations and then propose violent, illegal activities that cause the police to shut down the organization (Stauber and Rampton 1996). Corporations can offer employees paid time off to participate in seemingly civic associations to support the company's profit-making plans – so Best Buy, an electronic goods chain, got members of its tech repair team to come testify before Congress, in a colorful display, wearing their "Geek Squad" uniforms, to make sure that a policy that benefited Best Buy's profit margins passed (Walker forthcoming).

Why is this harmful and not just mildly amusing? First of all, wealthy donors could set up campaigns that are aimed to undermine real grassroots campaigns. This is what happened with activism around the issue of human rights in Burma. Protesters were concerned about human rights abuses in Burma, including the use of slave labor by some big foreign corporations. The activists tried to pass laws giving sanctions to companies that did business in Burma. Some of the corporations that benefited from Burmese slave labor rallied a group of fellow corporations in response. They set up a think tank called "Engage America" aimed at fighting the activists, and their work got results: courts decided that some of the human rights activists' successes were illegal and businesses should be entirely free to work in Burma, slaves and all (Dale 2010: 116–20). *Toxic Sludge is Good for You* provides many other examples of this process, in which corporations undermine real grassroots campaigns with fake grassroots campaigns.

Another reason that this process is scary and not just amusing is that these events' sponsors might consider it dangerous for participants to see the big picture, since these campaigns' whole purpose is to mask any bad smells that the sponsors might emit. A quick search online yielded some examples to me: Citigroup, one of the perpetrators of the world financial meltdown, sponsors a yearly "Global Community Day." Another perpetrator, Goldman Sachs, sponsored Community TeamWorks; Morgan Stanley sponsors both "What a Difference a Day Makes," and "Global Volunteer Month." BP sponsored the Gulf oil disaster, and also sponsors a toy drive and "Dress for Success," in which employees volunteer to collect business attire for low-income women in Houston, and a beach clean-up (in the bayou, not the Gulf, thank goodness!). Another event, "Big Sunday," is a big one-day volunteer event, sponsored by a nonprofit. It is not, itself, a corporation, but its website offers to "connect your publicity team with ours to maximize PR for your project." If a corporation is doing something harmful, the volunteers can put a happy face on it. When a volunteer group has a corporate sponsor, or is indirectly being used for corporate PR, could the group end up being publicly critical of the sponsor? Probably not. The ideal of civic associations was, once upon a time, that citizens in them would have creative, open-ended freedom, and that people could make the road by walking it. Here, there is one road that cannot be taken, even if participants might prefer it: any critique of corporate power has a big roadblock in front of it.

With enough money, a person can fund a think-tank – an academic or quasi-academic research organization – that will support the person's views, no matter how outlandish and unproven. Most spectacularly, two billionaires, the Koch brothers, have spent hundreds of millions of dollars on extreme-Right causes in the USA. They have vast wealth from oil and logging. Now, they engage in most of the above practices. They indirectly have funded the Tea Party, and a huge range of other causes. They also fund a think

tank at George Mason University, the Mercatus Center. One of
its economists challenged a proposal from the Environmental
Protection Agency to limit ground-level ozone (which can cause
asthma and other permanent respiratory problems), which is produced mainly by fossil fuels, a major source of the Koch brothers'
wealth. The economist said that the proposed rule did not take
the health benefits of smog into account. With more smog, there is
less sunlight, and therefore, less skin cancer! While this economist
was working the courts with legal challenges, the Koch brothers'
funds were paying for the judges to go on vacations to a ranch
in Montana. These judges ruled against environmental protection (though of course, they denied that their all expenses-paid
junket had any affect on their decision). The Koch brothers set
up another organization that manufactures doubt about environmental issues; while scientists overwhelmingly agree that climate
change is happening, the Koch brothers-funded organization sows
confusion among ordinary citizens, so that uniformed citizens start
to wonder if coal and oil are better for the environment than solar
or wind energy, and if pollution is good for your health (Oreskes
and Conway 2010). To top it off, the wealthy funders can give
their organization a confusing name: Citizens for the Environment
(Mayer 2010).

Altogether, this is a perfect illustration of an "Astroturf" campaign. Astroturf is the fake grass made of plastic cellophane that
can be rolled out instantly to create the appearance of grass. But it
has no roots. An Astroturf campaign is one in which wealthy corporations or individuals spend money to produce the appearance
of grassroots movement.

Someone might argue that the massive infusion of money does
not really matter. After all, there were, before the Koch brothers,
people who opposed minimum wage laws, environmental regulation, social security, gun control, and nearly all taxes. One of the
Koch brothers ran for office on such a platform in 1980. He lost.
This could seem to show that money does not buy votes. Funders
of Astroturf campaigns sometimes claim that all they are doing is
giving voice to the silent majority. They claim that their expenditure of hundreds of millions of dollars has no affect (see Stauber

and Rampton 1996). It may seem like a peculiar use of money, by people who believe that they deserve power because they are good at managing money.

Instead of "one person, one vote," these civic associations operate on the principle of "one dollar, one vote." This tendency has been made stronger since the rise of internet activism, which requires no more than a click for the activist. (Walker 2010). With the public relations industry using sophisticated techniques to propel these well-funded industry-driven grassroots campaigns, "it becomes exceedingly difficult to distinguish between types of participation that have true empowering potential from those that reinforce institutionalized practices in state and market organizations" (Walker 2010: 52). In other words, instead of challenging the power of big business, these Astroturf campaigns reinforce it, protesting in favor of "business as usual." Corporations, governments, and individuals – or any other entity with enough money – can hire consultants who know how to invite "civic participation" in ways that end up making the "participants" go along with whatever the company wants them to believe (Lee 2010; forthcoming 2013). We will come back to this in chapter 6, because sometimes, top-down efforts to inspire participatory democracy are, indeed, sincere, and it is very hard to distinguish between "real" and "fake" participation.

After all this, a person at the lower end of the social ladder might look up at these giants' mutual back-scratching and wonder why an ordinary, non-gargantuan person should bother with civic engagement. The field is increasingly populated by behemoths, not mere humans.

Why Do Non-Elites Tend to Vote Less and Participate Less?

Now that we have examined the field of civic associations – that is, how civic associations relate to one another on a playing field that includes the whole gamut of such associations – let us now turn to the question of the internal workings of any one civic association.

Overall, surveys show that the further down one goes down the social hierarchy, the less likely are people to participate in civic associations, voting, and other public affairs (Verba, Schlozmann, and Brady 1996). Furthermore, volunteer groups tend to be very socially homogeneous. A person usually joins an association when a current member invites him or her to a meeting. Since people tend to be friends with people they meet in their neighborhood, school, religious institution, or at work, the voluntary association tends to gather birds of a feather (McPherson and Smith-Lovin 1987). Associations provide grounds for networking, thus increasing the power of the powerful. The social conditions that produced such gaping inequalities need changing before "participation" can be meaningful. So, why don't poor people form their own associations to overturn this inequality? After all, there are more poor people than there are rich.

First of all, they sometimes do. Over the course of history, poor and barely literate people have eloquently spoken out against tyrants, able to imagine that "another world is possible" – as contemporary activists in the World Social Forum put it. Throughout history, there have been "world turned upside down" rituals, like medieval European parades, Mardi Gras, or carnivals, in which the lowliest person played the role of the king.

Furthermore, a certain, specific type of civic association clearly counterbalances a lack of elite status. Organizations that exist for the purpose of pressing for the rights of the disadvantaged – unions and political parties that represented the working class in most of the world during the 1900s (Bourdieu 1984), or groups of Latino high-school students who press for programs to help themselves (Terriquez, forthcoming; Noguera 2006) – can help disadvantaged people find a public voice. People who participate in these associations learn to think of themselves as qualified political participants, whose voices are just as important as elites', and whose ideas might be just as good. Working-class people in France, for example, used to be organized in working-class-based political parties, throughout the 1900s. As members of parties that highlighted their class interests, these non-elites voted as often as elites, answered public opinion surveys with just as few "don't knows" as elites, and potentially gained power as members of the oppressed category. Being in a class-based political party was like being in a "school for democracy" that was tailored to working-class members' questions, hopes, and needs (Bourdieu 1984).

When civic associations or political parties bring people together under auspices that are not based on members' shared oppression – helping lost dogs, for example, or choosing between one group of millionaires (Democrats) and another (Republicans) – participation does not have this empowering effect on non-elites. The members are coming together without an agenda that will address the most pressing issue for the disadvantaged members: the sources of their own disadvantage.

Still, people often continue for centuries undergoing outrageous oppression without rebelling. Why? One explanation is one that we have already revisited in this book: they are not accustomed to making decisions that affect other people on a large scale. It's the workers' plight in Tocqueville's "aristocracy of industry:" the people at the top learn to rule, as if over a vast kingdom, while the person who puts heads on pins all day learns to think about heads of pins, and becomes a pinhead. Such lowly citizens are not paid to think; they're paid not to think. Thinking might make them rebellious. This explanation attributes poor people's silence to the daily drudgery of everyday life. All day long, people see that life is, well, the way it is. They just assume that this is the only possible reality, according to this explanation. Some scholars, however, argue that oppressed people *have* often been able to imagine that another world is possible (Scott 1989; Eliasoph 1998; Gaventa 1982). The question is whether the people can *talk* about this imagination, so that each knows what the other is imagining, rather than assuming that it's each person's own dirty secret.

Another explanation for the silence of the downtrodden points to a "dominant ideology" that discourages people from thinking about ideas that might challenge the power structure. According to this perspective, the people who control economic production also control the production of ideas. In earlier eras, this meant that the king could convince everyone else that God himself appointed him to rule society and to eat roast suckling pig for dinner. Now, it means that the people at the top control the circulation of ideas in the public arena – in the news, in schools – teaching a lesson that proves that the people at the top deserve to be there, and the people at the bottom deserve to be there. Critics of this approach say that it is implausible because it assumes that people are almost brainwashed, as if to say that if workers are told that workers earn too much, they believe it. If they are told that anyone can get ahead if they work hard, they believe it. It is not usually the case.

Is the Absence of Protest Due to a Lack of Consciousness or a Lack of Appropriate Space for Communication?

Is it true that most people have a coherent set of ideas that convince them to accept the status quo? Not quite. Rather, people have a mishmash of mismatched ideas in their heads about politics. If a survey asks people if the boy born in the poorest neighborhood in their city and the kid born in the wealthiest neighborhood in their city have equal chances of getting ahead, many people say, "no." But if the question is reworded slightly, to ask if rich and poor have equal chances of getting ahead in this country, many of the *same people* say "yes" (Schuman and Presser 1997). As an abstract catechism, in theory, they agree with the idea, but when they imagine it for real, in their own town, they disagree. If they do not have a safe space for talking about the mismatch, they usually do not notice it. They would notice the disconnect only if they had to put it to the test, doing something practical with fellow citizens. This is the job of civic associations – to give people the conditions in which they have to put their ideas to the test. But underprivileged people are less likely to join associations than their privileged counterparts.

The problem is not just that lower-status people are less likely to join civic associations, but that they are less likely to speak in them when they do join. Why? People often have to work hard to suppress their political concern, so that they can avoid feeling discouraged. It might look like apathy, but it is not just a blank.

Most people are aware of social problems, but it is hard for them to find a *place* to give voice to their complaints and ideas.

"When the king goes by, the wise peasant bows deeply and silently farts." This is the epilogue for James Scott's book, *Domination and the Arts of Resistance*, about how the ideas of the ruling classes come to be "the ruling ideas" of a society (Scott 1989). Roving the planet across time and to every continent, spanning varied modern and pre-modern societies, the anthropologist concludes that it is *not* because the non-elites believe what their rulers tell them, but that oppressed people are prevented from speaking their voice in public. Speaking out can get them in trouble: they can lose their jobs, lose their land, lose their reputations, be shamed, be exiled, executed; above all and most likely, they can cause themselves extreme shame, if they think they have said something stupid.

Scott argues that not having free access to the public forum is, itself, a form of deprivation. A person who sees injustice and fears speaking out suffers not only from the injustice, but also from the inability to speak out. A careful study of an Appalachian mining valley and its seemingly acquiescent miners shows how this silence arises, over the course of generations of miners who find themselves in trouble when they try to make their voices heard. This study shows that the miners felt outrage, but expressed it in nearly invisible, inaudible ways, until they detected a faint possibility for hope. They expressed support for a newly open-minded union leadership for a moment, for example, but when the union went back to business as usual, the miners started *sounding* apathetic again (Gaventa 1982).

My own book, *Avoiding Politics*, also shows how people create this appearance of apathy. It takes a great deal of work to produce this public appearance of apathy. Volunteers in a group of parents of high-school students devoted themselves to raising funds for the school, and when they were in the group setting, they studiously avoided political conversation. Meetings were peppered with comments to one another like, "We're small but we're energetic! We accomplish a lot more than you'd think!" They had to keep a "can-do" spirit afloat, and they assumed that discussing big, political issues would crush it. So, participants focused their attention on smaller, more "do-able" projects like what kind of hot dog steamer to buy for fundraisers. The volunteers knew about nearby political problems, but could only talk about them outside of the group context – over breakfast in a group at a local diner, or in interviews, for example. Some topics that they mentioned in that context were, for example, the lack of funds that led to the school library's roof's caving in, the race riot at the school, pesticides in food, homelessness, the dangers of living between two large military bases, and the large toxic site in one of them, a mile away from the school. In interviews, it was clear that the parent volunteers did know and care about political issues; they just could not talk about them in the group setting. In an interview, for example, one parent volunteer who had just finished saying that she lived less than a mile from a major nuclear waste site, said, full of hesitation, "But I do feel powerless, so, I mean, in a sense. That's why, uh, I'm not worried about it, uh, nuclear power." But they could not bring themselves to *talk* about these issues in meetings or in activities related to the volunteer work, like while they were steaming those dogs. When they were wearing their volunteer "hats," they needed to keep up an upbeat, can-do spirit, which meant, to them, not talking about discouraging problems that they could not immediately solve with hands-on work. Talking about bigger issues would have been "inappropriate" and "out of place." But behind the scenes, "backstage," they *did* talk about the "bigger" issues.

Similarly, activists who were trying to prevent a toxic incinerator from being built in their city developed a sophisticated analysis of the problem. When they were just chatting informally, "backstage," they talked about the lack of government regulation, lack of pressure, sweetheart deals between government and corporate polluters, the fact that the US military is the world's largest producer of toxic waste, and that whatever their little local group did, they vowed *not* to be saying "Not In My Backyard." No, they did not want to be "NIMBYs" and get the waste put "in someone else's backyard." But when these same activists spoke, in front of the press, they would only speak about their own property values going down, their own children's health, their own pretty landscape that would be destroyed: they sounded narrower and more self-interested in public than they did when they were just chatting among themselves. They assumed that the public forum was a place for self-interested people to fight for what they want, not a place for people to discuss what would be good and just for the whole society. There was no decent place for them to speak out.

Finally, and probably most importantly, imagine being that ruddy fellow at the town meeting in the iconic image, while the suits listen patiently. What are you feeling? A political scientist (Mansbridge 1980) attended a series of such town meetings in Vermont in the 1970s and discovered that poor people, not surprisingly, rarely spoke, because of a deep sense of shame. They were ashamed at how inarticulate they might sound, and overwhelmed with fear that they might make fools of themselves in public. Interviewee Florence Johnson, for example, says that she does not speak up because she does not know enough. Perhaps she is too ignorant to speak intelligently, but other disadvantaged people might know quite a bit, and are still ashamed anyway. Whatever the reason for their silence, it becomes a spiral of silence, because the more ashamed they are to ask questions and speak out, the more their ideas and interests will be ignored, and the more their ideas and interests are ignored, the more distant and bewildered they will feel.

Speaking out in public is, for most people, uncomfortable. In one way, this is as it should be, if civic associations are supposed to help people challenge easy presuppositions (Schudson 1998). The question then, is not necessarily how to make speaking out just sweeter, smoother, nicer, and less challenging for everyone, but whether anything could help make level the playing field. What could make not just elites, but more ordinary people feel more able to speak about political controversies in public? That is our next chapter's topic.

6

Opening Up Civic Participation

What could make more people get more absorbed in public affairs and decision-making than they are now?

Trying to open up space for the widest range of viewpoints possible without becoming completely disorganized, civic associations and cities around the world have experimented with novel ways of running meetings and structuring a group. This final section of this book reports on some of these novel designs.

Before going to "novel" designs, let us revisit a tried and true old-fashioned solution.

Some volunteer projects bring many of empowerment projects' missions together, but only by dropping at least one of the components. Some volunteer programs heavily train, screen, and supervise volunteers, for example. The work is not transparently accountable to hurried, distant funders. For example, an observer spent two years visiting over one hundred settlement houses like Hull House, in the late 1950s, and described them in great detail (Hillman 1960). One was typical in the way it made use of volunteers to work with troubled families. First, prospective volunteers were interviewed – interrogated, is more like it – regarding their motives, their schedules, their long-term commitment, their husband's willingness (most of the volunteers were housewives, reflecting the norm at the time), their psychological fortitude and sensitivity. After that, one third of the prospective volunteers dropped out. The ones who stayed then had to take a course, and then, once they start working with the families, they had to have a debriefing session with a professional after each visit to the family. While not very many volunteers stuck it out, the ones who did were truly helpful. The volunteering becomes, in the words of one sociologist who studied these long-term, assiduous, unpaid women volunteers, an "invisible career" (Daniels 1988).

In other words, these projects were not transparently accountable on a short time line. These old-fashioned volunteers did not have "loose connections" (Wuthnow 1999; Lorentzen and Hustinx 2007) but connections that were more like the long-term, stable relationships of old-fashioned marriages and old-fashioned careers. If such volunteering is still possible, in some places and for some people, it seems worth trying, however quaint and old-fashioned it may seem.

Now, having honored a very respectable option that might only be something that most of us can look upon with nostalgia, let us turn to some more current experiments that aim to involve average citizens in decision-making about their local, national, and global societies.

Consensus and Leaderlessness Groups

The standard style for organizing a civic group in the USA calls for the group to elect a president, vice-president, secretary, and the rest. Activists have criticized this style for being too hierarchical, saying that when only some people can be leaders, the others do not get to take full advantage of the process of civic association. Some activists in the 1960s thus preferred *leaderless groups.* Unfortunately, the result was often a "tyranny of structurelessness," according to one observer. There *were* leaders, but they were not elected. Instead, they operated as a social clique, and their informal decision-making excluded people who were not part of their social circle (Freeman 1972). Furthermore, when organizations did not select their own leaders through a group decision-making process such as voting, the media selected the organizations' leaders for them. Student anti-war activists in the 1960s were often in the news, and reporters had to find people to interview. When the movement itself did not pick spokespeople, how could reporters decide whom to interview? The reporters usually found people who seemed like the reporters' image of real leaders – tall, male, and from an elite university, for example (Gitlin 1980).

The Occupy movement has faced a similar set of dilemmas. Movement members do not want leaders, but then there is the problem of representing the movement to the rest of the public. Anti-nuclear activists in the 1970s and 1980s often solved this problem by appointing *spokespeople* who were not *leaders* (Epstein 1993; Lichterman 1996). The *spokesperson* was someone whom other group members trusted to represent the group, but she or he was not a *leader*. In some of these organizations, the spokesperson had to say precisely what the group authorized him or her to say, no more, no less. This constrains the creativity of the spokesperson, but it avoids the risk of appointing a spokesperson who slyly becomes a leader, on the one hand, and the risk of letting the media just appoint whatever nutcase they want to speak for the movement, on the other hand.

Another variation of group structure is *consensus decision-making*. It is aimed at inviting more people's voices to be part of the decision-making process, and producing more thoughtful discussion. In the standard civic association, the group makes a decision by holding a short discussion and then voting – be it about which hot-dog roaster to buy, whether to stage a sit-in, or whether to join forces with a like-minded group. In this standard kind of group, the majority rules, and decisions can usually be made quickly, with little or no discussion.

Consensus decision-making works differently. Ideally, the issue is discussed long enough for everyone to agree, or at least not to "block consensus." If a majority favors a decision, but a strong minority disagrees, the group goes back to discussion. In some versions of consensus decision-making, even one person who feels strongly enough about an issue can block consensus.

There are some drawbacks to this process. One is that it is easy for any infiltrator or nitpicker to block or delay decisions. To overcome this drawback, various consensus decision-making protocols have different ways of finally arriving at decisions. The Occupy Wall Street movement used a guide book that organizations in Spain developed, which have a way of signaling "weak" support, and sometimes, a way of excluding a position that only one person holds (Occupy Wall Street 2012). But whatever consensus-based groups do, it is rarely as fast as in the standard, voting, "majority rules" group. As Francesca Polletta's realistically titled book *Freedom is an Endless Meeting* shows, such an organization comes to decisions slowly, but the decisions it arrives at are more binding and powerful. Every member has heard people imagine all the possible paths that any one decision might open up for the group.

Safe Spaces – Political Activism as Self-Exploration

Despite the slowness and other foibles of the consensus process, there is another reason that some organizations choose consensus decision-making over other decision-making techniques. When a group starts to open up the decision-making process this way, it can start to become a cross between an activist group and a self-help, consciousness-raising group. People writing about feminist and anti-racist organizations in the 1970s and 1980s, for example, described them as "safe spaces" in which participants could not just make decisions about what to *do* together, but create a shared sense of who to *be* together – of what it means to be "a woman," or "African American" or whatever other identity brought them together (Gamson 1996; Polletta 2002). They already knew what they had been told about what "being a woman" meant, but in a "safe space," they could redefine it for themselves.

Being a member of such a group can, according to these writers, become a process of self-discovery (Morgan 1979). This is different from "finding yourself" all by yourself. In a safe space, participants find what they share with others. The "aha" moment takes the form of "Oh, I thought it was just me! I thought I was the only one who had that experience/felt that/thought that!" These activist-self-help groups differ from solitary soul-searching in another way, too; the lone individual would have a hard time making his or her vague ideas have any real consequences for how people act.

One problem with "safe spaces" is that they assume that all members that share x characteristic also share y characteristic. After feminist groups jelled in the 1980s, women started to realize that women of different races, classes, sexual preferences, religions, and the rest had very different experiences. It could become a new form of oppression if one had to correspond to the average woman's experience, if one was not from a statistically typical background – if one came from a very poor or very wealthy family, or was a lesbian, for example. Forming new "safe spaces" based on women's differences posed another problem: Gloria Anzaldua, a working-class, Latina lesbian, for example, tells about first discovering feminism. In women's groups, she discovered that being female wasn't enough to bring her together with all other women. Being from a disadvantaged background made her life different from elite women's. But in groups with disadvantaged women, she discovered that being a disadvantaged feminist wasn't enough. Being Latina made her life different from the disadvantaged white feminists' lives. But in groups with Latinas, she discovered that being a disadvantaged, Latina feminist still wasn't enough. Being a disadvantaged Latina lesbian feminist made her life different from other Latinas (Anzaldua 1992). Often, these different "differences" map onto one another; most Latinas come from disadvantaged backgrounds at that time, for example. Still, one can imagine keeping on going till one would need a safe space with only oneself in it.

Internet Activism

The internet has become more than a means of communication; it has become a site of activism itself. When a potential volunteer or activist is looking for a group to join, or the next meeting time, she or he usually looks online. Many people have online relationships that feel just as real to them as their face-to-face relationships. Now online, the potential activist can not only find the schedule for the next face-to-face event, but can participate straightaway in a blog or repost material from the organization's website onto Facebook. Being a group member now often includes the person's online presence. Some organizations devote huge amounts of time to their web presence, as I discovered when volunteering for the Los Angeles County Bike Coalition where I found myself creating audio feeds for its website while in the office listening to office conversation that mostly revolved around the organization's website, Twitter, Facebook, and other social media platforms.

Arguments abound regarding the political importance of this technology. Francesca Polletta et al. (forthcoming) neatly summarize some: On the one hand, the barriers to involvement are lower. A person can participate anonymously, so embarrassment is not as likely. Florence Johnson, the woman in the Vermont town meeting who was afraid to speak up for fear of sounding stupid, might dare write a sentence or two. The other side of this debate says that the goods that Tocqueville said come from civic engagement – learning to think, learning to feel, and learning to self-organize and take power – do not seem obviously to emerge from a point and click motion. It could become another form of mindless consumerism, or a way of "branding" oneself.

Another debate concerns the top-down nature of many online campaigns. The Obama campaign hired experts in web design to figure out which exact shade of deep blue would work best for the Obama website, and told "grassroots" activists exactly how to participate to muster votes for the 2008 election. In this case, were the local activists autonomously creating the kind of civic associations that Tocqueville dreamed would make democracy work? No, the activists were small pieces of a big machine (Kreiss 2012). When the machine was effective, did it promote democracy? The observer tends to say yes when she or he agrees with the resulting victory, for Obama in this case, but if the other side used the same techniques, the same observer would object.

Another debate about internet-based activism started before the internet developed and now is all the more relevant. This is about the importance of face-to-face camaraderie as opposed to communication at a distance. Some political organizations, like

Greenpeace, exist mainly as lobbying groups, and to "join," you write a check. It is hard to find a local meeting of those groups, so some scholars argue that they are hollowing out civic life (Skocpol 2003). If people don't meet up in flesh and blood, they won't feel the fellow feelings that civic associations can offer, and they won't learn civic skills, either. Other scholars disagree, saying that just learning that there *are* other people who think or feel the way you do – even if those people are far away – can make you brave enough to talk politics locally. The argument started before the internet. Now, it is hard to separate one's "online self" from one's "offline self." Partly because of this newly "dispersed" selfhood, a person can identify as, for example, gay or lesbian and feel okay about it even if he or she does not personally know any other LGBT people (Minkoff 2002).

Another debate about internet activism carries over from the pre-internet days. Much of what happens online is in the form of play, self-revelation (often revealing a self through a fictive online persona), not the serious, plodding debate that one imagines in a classic political meeting. There is the possibility of politicizing more of one's life, then (Hermes 2006). By going to a website to test their carbon footprint, consumers can play a game to learn what kind of damage they did to the environment when they bought those prawns that were grown in flooded mangrove swamps in Thailand and flown to their local grocery store (Luque 2005). Consumption becomes a political question. This possibility brings us to our next site of possible politicization.

Corporate Social Responsibility and Fair Trade

CSR and Fair Trade are two other worldwide attempts at re-jigging the relation between market, government, and civic association. "The triple bottom line" for corporations that engage in a "CSR" or fair trade agenda is: profit, planet, and people. The idea is that a corporation that treats its workers well and treats the planet well can also enjoy decent profits. To become "certified," a company fills out a long questionnaire, detailing their wages, family leave plans, environmental practices, and more – depending on the type of CSR involved. Independent inspectors come to check on the company's practices. Some CSR programs are stronger than others.

There is a great deal of controversy about it. Some people say the whole concept is an oxymoron. If, for example, Coca-Cola in South Africa produces Coke in a socially responsible way, what could that mean – that it bottles up something nutritious and useful, like soymilk, instead of Coke? What if Coca-Cola in South America is meanwhile suppressing unions, as some say it is? When chicken is fairly traded, did the chicken find it fair? Companies engage in CSR when it will improve their image (Lim 2012; Walker forthcoming). Some people say governments should be making laws about things like workplace safety, environmental protection, child labor, and the rest. They say these issues are too important to be regulated by voluntary, NGO-based programs that companies can *choose* to adopt.

Is it therefore nothing but a new, clever form of advertising? Several scholars say no, not always. It can, in some conditions, be much more than that. Alwyn Lim, for example, shows that one way that some companies become certified as "socially responsi-ble" is to allow political activists to inspect the shop floor, to see what working conditions really are like. Here is a very big chal-lenge to our previous assumptions about the relations between, and divisions between, market, state, and civic association: nor-mally, we expect governments to inspect companies. How does it differ if activists do it? It depends on which government and which activists, but when activists can publicize violations world-wide, there is a new balance between the three forces. If we come to a time in which people routinely look for the triple bottom line when producing and consuming, then will we have "humanized" the market (Lim 2012)? Or will we have just collapsed the distance between our "market" selves and our real "selves" that we think we have to buy a decaf soy latte made with fairly traded organic coffee at Starbucks to be a good person, as theorist Slavoj Žižek argues (http://www.youtube.com/watch?v=hpAMbpQ8J7g)?

Participatory Democracy Forums, Participatory City Budgets

Many cities and some regions have experimented in participatory democracy. These involve ordinary citizens coming together to discuss an issue together and arrive at a decision that policy-makers will have to consider. The title of one study asks the big question, "But Is It for Real?" (Lang 2007). The "but" in the title is brilliant; it reflects most people's preconception. Many people assume that it will fake. Among other assumptions that Caroline Lee describes in a study of such forums (Lee forthcoming) are the impressions that the people who can afford to sponsor these events are elites, who

- will not give participants real power, but will only listen to opinions that support what the elites wanted to do in the first place; and/or
- will not really give people enough time or unbiased information to arrive at a good decision; and/or
- will let people blow off steam without actually putting their suggestions into practice; and/or
- will give people a choice between painting the walls ultramarine blue or sky blue but not give them the power to make any more important decisions.

It is very difficult to distinguish between "real" and "fake" participatory democracy efforts. Many nonprofit and for-profit firms sell their trademarked processes of deliberation to companies and cities that want more participation. One such firm in the USA tells big corporations that its approach "heightens energy, sharpens vision and *inspires action for change without resistance*" (Lee 2010: 32 [with Lee's italics]). A British study of government-sponsored participatory forums reports that after participants went through the participatory process, they "expressed a willingness to cut several high-cost areas of expenditure, such as highways maintenance, libraries, museums, and residential services for older people" (Zacharzewski 2010: 5; quoted in Lee 2010: 31–2). This danger seems clear.

Another danger is that when there are no old people who need services in the "participatory" decision-making group, it might be easy to be blind to their needs and cut their services. Another risk is that the forum might just be set up to be a place for people to vent and to "feel their feelings," as Lee shows was the case in an expensive series of one-day annual post-Hurricane Katrina's participatory forums. These techniques for participation could colonize free-wheeling conversation. The one free space left for citizens to cultivate ideas that elites had not fed them would be destroyed. The only organizations that can hire these expert facilitators of "participation" are those that can afford it. So, if ordinary citizens start to expect this to be the normal form for participation, it could erode any chances for truly grassroots engagement, and undermine civic associations' powers in a way that goes far beyond Tocqueville's bad dream of an overly intrusive state. But it wouldn't be primarily the state that was doing the colonizing; it would be whatever unelected entities could afford the expert facilitators. More and more often, corporations are catching onto the importance of funding these kinds of short-term forums and splashy events (Walker forthcoming).

Such forums could be lavish propaganda campaigns, in other words, that make politicians and corporate sponsors look good while not actually doing any of the projects that participants suggest. Indeed, many organizers of these forums say that the process is as important, or more important, than any result. Their main agenda is often to encourage people just to open up their imaginations and envision change. But an abstract vision of change depends on a concrete implementation. Indeed, the concrete implementation is often really all that matters. For example, everyone wants better schools. So, when participants say they want better schools, everyone can agree with this as an abstract idea. But the trick is to implement policies that will get us there, and that is where all the disagreements arise. If, after a long process, participants discover that they favor good education, they still probably disagree on how to get there: More funding? Less funding and more voluntary parental involvement? More equality so that schools in poor neighborhoods get as much funding as schools in rich ones, which is not now the case in the USA? More testing? Less testing? Harsher punishments for violations of school policies? School uniforms? More shared core curriculum? More electives? These forums are rarely equipped to figure out such details, but just to get people to find agreement. These experiments often focus on learning a democratic "process" so that people can learn the art of decision-making, using their imaginations, finding agreement, and this is, indeed, one set of elements of active citizenship. But these projects are often disconnected from making the changes stick. If "democracy" means only "a process" and not a set of "outcomes" – a better, more humane society – no one will care if it dies.

Another danger is that the forum could focus people's attention on a small local problem without asking about its root cause, when the root cause might be the national or global policies of the past three decades that have given a great deal more wealth to the top one percent, while the assets of the bottom 99 percent shrink. So, government services must be cut, to continue to fund this upward sweep of wealth toward the wealthy. When cities worldwide are cutting services, inviting tightly controlled participation can become, as the British report cited earlier advertises, a very cost-effective and efficient way of "plucking more feathers without as much squawking" (Zacharzewski, cited in Lee 2010). Starting with a solution – cutting senior care, for example – without asking about the cause might short-circuit the debate right where it needs to start.

Could these participatory democracy projects *ever* work well, then, to promote real, creative, thoughtful public-spirited decision-making? The most famous among these experiments is Porto Alegre, Brazil, a city of a million people, and the answer seems to be, in this city, "yes." A surprisingly large portion of the population is involved in a very complex, complicated, and time-consuming process of determining the entire city budget. This city has become a veritable mecca for people who want to see how participatory democracy can really work. Thus, it has inspired much controversy, as well: do the poorest of the poor participate? Do middle-class, educated people get heard more than less elite participants? Does anyone fall through the cracks altogether? Do people make good decisions or do they just waste money on useless things?

Several studies show Porto Alegre's great success. They show that this process does arrive at better decisions than small elites in other cities reach. The participatory decisions improve the city's economy in a way that benefits more people than other forms of city government have. These studies also show that participation is much more equally distributed among the city's classes than anyone would have dreamed of predicting (Baiocchi 2002; Bacque and Sintomer 2001; Gret and Sintomer 2005). Other cities have tried adopting this process, but in much more limited ways. Some cities in Belgium, Spain, Italy, and France have it (Berger 2011) on a small scale. Los Angeles has a token bit of money available for Neighborhood Councils, but not enough to build half a block of road. Needless to say, with this tokenistic amount of money and lack of clear structure, Los Angeles' local decision-making just gets people organized to demand funding for their particular neighborhood's project, and thus reproduces the inequalities that already existed (Musso et al. 2006).

These successful empowerment projects differ from fake ones in predictable ways. First, *money* is not scarce. Surprisingly for people who welcome civic engagement as a way to cut costs, these projects include substantial government investment and oversight (Fung and Wright 2003).

Time is also not scarce; these projects do not operate on the short time lines of some of the empowerment projects described in chapter 4, and are never just one-day affairs like the ones Caroline Lee describes. Like old-fashioned volunteers, the ones who participate effectively in these projects invest huge amounts of time in a process that is funded well enough for participants to be able to be pretty sure that their decisions will have an effect. The Chicago school curriculum was redone partly by the work of some volunteers who committed themselves to a eighteen hours of training, after which they could make decisions within very strict parameters regarding what students should learn when (Fung 2003: 120). A similar program in India demands stepped levels of training depending on the decision-making power that the participant has: twenty days of training for some, ten for others, and "only" five for others (Thomas Isaac and Heller 2003: 83).

These "real" empowerment projects differ from the fake forums that Lee describes, or from most of the empowerment projects described in chapter 4 in another way as well: their *acknowledgment of complexity*. Part of what makes Porto Alegre's participatory budget succeed is precisely its complex, arduous process. If, as Baiocchi describes, a resident wants to work on the transportation committee and specialize in questions of road-building, he or she has to learn about the different properties of cement versus asphalt versus macadam paving, for example, as well as learning a precise format for making appeals for money. The participant has to be a trainee for a long time, before actually getting to make decisions. As Fung puts it in a description of how community policing and community school reforms in Chicago, "Only those with an abiding concern are likely to join these efforts ... The ideal of participation would not be one in which every citizen deliberates every issue, but in which everyone seriously deliberates something" (Fung 2003: 132).

All of these projects also include a high level of *conflict*, and unlike fake empowerment projects, participants in these do not ignore, but acknowledge and work through their conflicts. A series of "mutual qualification" sessions in France and the Netherlands involves not just learning a lot of rules, like the curriculum redesign did, but also enduring explosive emotional conflicts. These mutual qualification projects drew administrators and ghetto-dwellers into a series of meetings to discuss issues like discrimination on public transportation and access to public housing. The residents had to learn how to understand policy-making, and the policy-makers had to understand what it is like to live in a ghetto: thus, they "mutually" qualify each other (Carrel 2012). An in-depth study comparing participatory city projects in Spain, France, and Italy (2006, 2007) found the same thing that the mutual qualification project found regarding the importance of airing conflicts. Empowerment projects have to acknowledge conflict if they hope to empower people in any enduring way. This means risking exposing people to embarrassment and shame in public, he says, but the positive side to this is that the people who do not get scared off become very competent, dedicated civic participants. Surely, there are ways to minimize the risks of public humiliation while preserving the openness to conflict; but, as Talpin (2007) notes, just avoiding conflict altogether makes it impossible for empowerment projects to empower anybody.

Finally, there is something that cannot be orchestrated from above in all of these situations: in most of the empowerment projects just described, in the Indian state of Kerala, in Porto Alegre, in the cities Talpin studied in Spain, France, and Italy, there was already a long *tradition* of overt political conflict, and a well-established Left that ensured that decisions were slanted toward benefitting the least advantaged (Gret and Sintomer 2005). Only Chicago lacked this pre-existing Leftist political culture, though it has had a stronger tradition of unions and political activism than most American cities and suburbs (Oliver 2001). In other words, people entered these projects already equipped with a "big picture" social vision, so they would not just clamor for more advantages to go to the already-advantaged.

Time, money, acknowledgment of complexity and *of conflict*, and a *political culture* that gives people a big picture in the first place: these five elements potentially transform band-aid solutions of the sort Lee describes into genuinely empowering projects. Even then, one would still want to know how these projects addressed the dilemmas described in chapter 4. For example, in the Chicago school reform projects, each local group was very strictly accountable to authorities, and the core goal was to raise standardized test scores. So one wonders if there is an abiding tension between the empowerment project's missions of appreciating local, grassroots uniqueness versus being transparent to multiple distant audiences.

We come full circle here, back to the settlement houses described at the beginning of this chapter: to have the time to invest in such big projects, citizens need . . . time and money! They cannot be running to their second low-paid job, cannot be spending time driving their children to distant private schools to mop up for poor public schools, cannot be working harder and harder each year just to stay in place. Some greater entity – usually the state – has to invest in ensuring that these forms of civic engagement really work. In other words, the balance between "civic," "state" and "market" would have to shift, so that more people had more free time. Here we are at that utopian vision of the mid twentieth century: that when technology makes people more and more productive, they will have to work less, and can participate in decision-making more. Their utopia didn't materialize, but it might not be too late. Having to work less will not, all by itself, make people into active citizens, but at least it won't prevent them from becoming active citizens.

Conclusion: Is Democracy in Our Future?

This book has described some trends in civic engagement over the past decades. Vast concentrations of wealth are flowing upwards, more than at any other time since 1929, the year the stock market crashed. So, most people have less time and energy to devote to decision-making about common affairs. There are, at the same time, new kinds of participation in the form of one-day facilitated public engagement projects, and corporate-sponsored two-hour-long volunteer opportunities, as well as a few scattered long-term, thoughtful engagements. A related transformation is that whereas before, there were long-term ties, now there are "loose connections" that are short-term and not deeply part of the volunteer's identity. Another transformation is what scholars and practitioners call "the NGO-ization" or "hybridization" of civic engagement; volunteering no longer mainly takes place in Tocquevillean voluntary associations (Edwards 2012; Eliasoph 2009).

After reading about all the potential failures of democracy described in this book, it is easy to imagine dystopias. Each chapter conjures up more than one. The first chapter lists five all by itself, when it describes Tocqueville's nightmares. The second chapter implies two complementary nightmares, when volunteering and politics detach from one another. The chapter on the balance between market, state, and civic life portrays a very precarious tripod; at any moment, democracy can go off balance and collapse. The chapter on empowerment projects shows one dilemma after another, and the chapter on inequality shows many factors that discourage disadvantaged people's political voice and vastly amplify the voices of the wealthy. Even the chapter on hopeful experiments shows dangers, as greedy and power-hungry people try to take over every new experiment, ten minutes after it is invented, if not earlier. One clear point after all this is that democracy is a constant experiment, and there will never be one equilibrium that could just settle things once and for all. Clever but selfish people will always try to undermine it, and depending on how well the rest of us can protect democracy, the selfish people might prevail.

The easiest dystopia to imagine could combine elements from all of the dire predictions. It is really easy to imagine this dystopia, because parts of it already exist. In our easy-to-imagine, close-at-hand dystopia, there would be an extreme concentration of wealth and power in private hands, and very little wealth for the rest of the population. We can remember the image painted in chapter 1, of the billionaire in the Eastern European republic of Georgia, Bidzina Ivanishvili, who controls more of the nation's wealth than the government itself, while the vast majority of Georgians live in poverty. Were such unequal fortunes to be the norm in a once-democratic nation, democracy would collapse (Walzer 1980). The handful of people who controlled the majority of the nation's wealth would control the nation. The rest of the people would be too bedraggled and exhausted to take care of the society, after trying to put bread on the table.

To make such unequal conditions palatable to us, the plebs, and make it all seem like it still really was democracy, the billionaires could claim to be "empowering" us. They could invite us to "visioning" sessions, and could give us crayons and magic markers to help us free our imaginations. When we decided that we want better schools (rather than wanting worse ones!), they could thank us for our creative input. This training in mutual self-deception could begin in early childhood, so that it became part of our very sense of self.

Combined with this, grassroots people, from the bottom up, could find teeny-tiny outlets for their natural compassion. They could become politically passive volunteers, lending a helping hand to mop up after socially created, unnecessary human suffering and ecological destruction. Detaching themselves from any political critique, the volunteers in the nightmare could, for example, feed and house the poor after powerful corporations and neglectful governments had left them hungry and homeless. The compassionate volunteers could heroically rescue individual fluffy animals whose entire habitats had been destroyed by industry or by global climate change or by poverty, when poor people take over land that the animals needed. The volunteers could tenderly feed each animal with a bottle, raise it in a human-made environment, and forget about the whole rest of the creature's habitat.

There could, in the nightmare, still be some large-scale *causes célèbres*, when movie stars and sports heroes take on a pet issue. Suddenly, for a few weeks, everyone would be talking about seals (but not walruses, which are less adorable) and one ethnic group that needed food (but not the one next door, whose members had worse clothes or less skilled publicists). Campaigns like the one in spring of 2012 about Invisible Children could spread quickly, if the ad makes the issue look easy enough to digest quickly. Each citizen's inbox could be deluged with a bewildering, overwhelming cascade of such good causes, each separate from the other. You could choose either to care about seals or Ogoni people, but not both at once. You would have to choose two or three NGOs to which to devote your attention, time, and money, but could not ask how or if there was any connection between the destruction of one habitat and the other, or between unequal power relations and habitat destruction, or wonder if any law could prevent future destruction rather than just trying to clean up after it's too late.

In this dystopia, ordinary citizens could start to notice that they had almost no power and could just retreat into their own private worlds, as Tocqueville worried. But there could be an even more terrifying scenario: ordinary citizens could *not notice* their powerlessness. When Citibank sponsored Global Community Day, and Goldman Sachs sponsored Community TeamWorks, and BP sponsored a beach clean-up, bands of clean and merry volunteers could feel really proud of having put in a healthy day's work doing good community service. They could do this without even asking if their corporate sponsors were using their volunteer work for PR, to cover up bank failures and oil spills. The volunteers could be like the "little platoons" that Republican leaders said were the backbone of democracy – little elves who followed commands with great cheer (quoted in Beem 1999).

If, despite all this, citizens still rose up to protest something a corporation was doing, the corporations could organize its corporation-friends to form a counter organization, like Engage*America, described in chapter 5.

If exhortations to engage in more volunteering usually went hand-in-hand with government cutbacks for social services and/or corporate PR, then people would start to roll their eyes when they heard words like "participation" and "civic engagement." The politicians' and corporations' rallying cry for "civic engagement" would easily just start to seem like propaganda for government cost-cutting and corporate executives' profit-making. It could make government leaders look like they cared, while their policies made people suffer. The leaders would be asking volunteers to solve problems that are too big.

Even if, for example, every Georgian volunteered, Bidzina Ivanishvili would run the show in his small nation republic. If he did not consider it to be important for children to have health care, no amount of volunteering in this rather impoverished nation could fill the gap between the need and the capacity to fulfill it. If Bidzina Ivanishvili did not want to spend money on creating safe working conditions in his companies, no amount of volunteer work could bring safety. One would need a state for that, but since Bidzina Ivanishvili could outspend the state, he could create propaganda persuading voters not to vote, or not to vote for health and safety, if he so desired. Or, as has happened in reality, Bidzina Ivanishvili could decide to run for office and he would probably win, because he could outspend all opponents, unless there were strict laws regulating campaign financing. Have we arrived at dystopia already?

No Choice But to Choose (and to keep hope alive)

This book's assertion has been that ordinary mortals can make binding decisions for each other, in a meaningful, non-tokenistic way. Some civic associations are old-fashioned grassroots movements of unpaid people banding together to accomplish something that they consider important for the greater good of society. While you may disagree with them – pro-choice, pro-life; pro-immigrants' rights, anti-immigration; Occupy and Arab Spring movements might be some candidates – they often force you, the observer, to ask why the activists feel so strongly about their cause. Grassroots engagement also appears when simple volunteers do the kinds of hands-on care-giving that does not claim to "empower" anybody or to improve society, but operates on another level, as person-to-person compassion. This is a noble activity, though, as we have seen throughout this book; if we want to *prevent* the woes that caused the need for volunteers to begin with, we often have to look beyond personal care-giving to find out why it was missing in the first place.

Other civic engagement takes the form of NGOs and empowerment projects of various forms. All over the world, people are conducting experiments aimed at inducing more civic engagement. While some of them are cynical PR efforts, many are not. Sometimes, they empower people, and sometimes, they have the opposite effect, and often, there is a mix of the two. The previous chapter has shown some ways of distinguishing between these organizations' potentials: They need time. They need money, usually from a state that can finance empowerment projects over the long haul and without having one company's financial interests at stake. They need to acknowledge complexity, and conflict. And they need somehow to create a culture that allows people to see the big picture and sometimes stand aside, to affirm decisions that help people who are more disadvantaged than they themselves may be. So, if you are looking for a place to volunteer, expect a long-term commitment, and expect to feel perplexed and even dizzy for a while, as you learn to see the big picture, with all its complexities and conflicts. And be on guard about who is sponsoring your project.

Democracy forces you to question your cherished ideas about human nature – your "common sense." What the "modern" thinkers of the past imagined as a dream – a society whose members *decide* how to live together – is now the *only* choice (Giddens 1991). We *have* to choose how to live together because there are so many different possibilities all in any one city, when people and words can move around the planet so easily. We *have* to choose because the market now is powerful enough to take over even more of life than ever before. While several centuries ago, no one had even seriously considered privately owning land, we now can turn genes, seeds, uteruses, and all sorts of care-giving and knowledge-producing devices into commodities that can be sold, rented, or patented. Since so much of our "common sense" comes from uninspected ideas about the unequivocal centrality of market life, we have to take an inventory of our beliefs about the market.

We *have* to choose for another reason. There are no longer any places untouched by social decision-making. If we don't choose to protect the planet, we will burn up and die of thirst. Northern Norwegian farmers once could trust their ancient wisdom, passed down through dozens of generations, about when to plant which crop. Each year, they have to plant their crops earlier, in response to global climate change (Norgaard 2011). There is nowhere far away enough to run. Similarly, Inuit cultural tradition used to be harmonious with their natural environment. Now,

> The Inuit diet of "country food" which includes marine mammals such as beluga whale, narwhal, and seal, puts them at the top of a contaminated food chain. The toxins collect in the animals' fat and are passed on to the Inuit as they eat, or through breast milk. The bodies of Arctic people, particularly Greenland's Inuit, contain the highest human concentrations of POPs (a toxic chemical residue) found anywhere on Earth – levels so extreme that the breast milk and tissues of some Greenlanders could be classified as hazardous waste. (from Bluevoice.org, 7/12/05)

The Inuit's "natural," traditional diet, rich in seal fat, now concentrates toxins from around the world, so it is not clear which to count as natural. "Nature" becomes for us a project and a research question, rather than the eternal ground beneath our feet. Nature starts to seem more and more like the sediment of centuries of human, political decisions.

So, we have to decide, and we all secretly know it. Pretending to separate the fate of the planet from the fate of individuals becomes less and less plausible. How do we decide? It is always tempting to say, when confronted with a new idea about how to organize a seemingly natural social institution like the market, the state, civic association, religion, or family, "This change won't work because human nature is basically x, y, or z," with our usual candidates being "lazy, greedy, and/or competitive."

But humans, unlike other creatures, have the capacity consciously to create the world in which we live. Lacking fur, claws, wings, scales, fangs, anything else that might allow us to survive through instinct, we have to rely on each other. Even the most basic biological drives come to us only after having been kneaded, cooked, decorated, and processed in every which way, differently in each society. Lots of other animals can build shelters, for example, but bees cannot decide to build sparkling modern hives whose plate-glass windows have views of thousands of other hives' twinkling lights, fueled by electricity that has traveled on power lines from a thousand miles away. Bees don't consciously choose to build some high-rise hives and some cozy wooden hives with braided rugs, and bees cannot make their entire hive fly, as we can, when we fly ourselves to the moon.

This book is not about sex, unfortunately, but sexuality provides a good illustration of human nature's wily essence: yes, we all need a sperm and an egg to reproduce, but beyond that, societies have endlessly, wildly varying rules, about how and when and with whom to have sex – doing it in pairs or in harems; for love or not; consensually or not; with relatives or not, and if so, which ones; and whether reproduction must be connected to sex, and if so, if it should be at age ten or thirty-five. In some societies, it is mandatory for a girl to do it with her uncle, as an initiation into the arts of love before marriage (Berger and Luckmann 1966). Like sexuality, compassion is part of every society, but it appears in wildly different forms and with wildly different effects in different societies. If this is true of sex, which is an eternal, biological drive, then how much more true is it of something as new and puzzling as "civic engagement?"

Compassion is another example of a seemingly obvious drive that has been around for all of human history. This book's question has been how to make compassion easier for most people to act on more often, and, equally importantly, how to build compassion into routine social structure so that being compassionate does not feel like shoveling sand against the tide. Compassion, curiosity, creativity, greed, selfishness, laziness – any number of seemingly natural, seemingly eternal features of humankind look as if they explain our ability, or lack of ability, to self-organize. Common sense says that they are all just human nature. Here again, the idea of civic engagement is that all societies amplify some basic drives and squash others. Our society already amplifies greed compared to most other societies in human history, for example, but it was not a policy we decided upon together, intentionally.

Our decisions about how to fabricate our lives together rarely feel like decisions, but even entrenched customs sometimes come up for public questioning. As we have seen, customs about gender relations and physical disabilities are two of the most spectacular examples of the past decades. The only sure thing that is really "human nature" is your social being. You are surrounded by human creations, and your ways of loving, desiring, hating, knowing how to do things and to think, imagine, and believe are shaped by the world we create together. If you don't shape it, someone else will do it for you.

The promise of civic engagement has been that people can think together about how to organize their shared world, rather than pretending to rely on a solid bedrock of some imagined, fictitious "human nature." The agenda is to figure out how to organize our shared lives together in a way that could realistically create a world that will, in turn, create our best "selves." Civic associations, whether in the workplace or after-hours, provide one place for people to learn how. If they are deprived of the chance to practice these arts, they are deprived of the very thing that lets them grow up, to become truly human adults (Erikson 1959). This is remarkable. It means that we, in the past couple of centuries, can become a different kind of fully adult person from the person that people in earlier eras could become. People are always inventing new forms of togetherness; humans now have invented the idea of civic association. Now that we have the idea, we can use it, and *for the first time in history*, we, in the twenty-first century, know that our decisions and actions will affect the future possibilities for life on earth.

References

Addams, Jane. 1960 [1910]. *Twenty Years at Hull-House*. New York: Signet.

Addams, Jane. 2002 [1901]. *Democracy and Social Ethics*. Urbana: University of Illinois Press.

Addams, Jane. 2005 [1909]. *The Spirit of Youth and the City Streets*. Gloucester, UK: Dodo Press.

Adler, Gary. 2012. *Encountering Distant Suffering: the Culture, Production, and Outcomes of Transnational Immersion Trips Along the U.S.–Mexico Border*. Doctoral thesis. Tucson: University of Arizona, Department of Sociology.

Al-Daini, Adnan. 2011. "David Cameron and the 'Happiness Index'" *Huffington Post*, Aug 1, 2011, http://www.huffingtonpost.co.uk/adnan-aldaini/david-cameron-and-the-hap_b_914218.html.

Anzaldua, Gloria. 1992. *Borderlands*. San Francisco, CA: Aunt Lute Press.

Appiah, Kwame Anthony. 2010. *The Honor Code: How Moral Revolutions Happen*. New York: W.W. Norton.

Bacque, Hélène, and Yves Sintomer. 2001. "Gestion de proximité et démocratie participative." *Les Annales de la recherche urbaine* 90: 148–55.

Bagdikian, Ben. 1997. *The Media Monopoly*. Boston: Beacon Press.

Baiocchi, Gianpaolo. 2002. *Militants and Citizens*. Stanford: Stanford University Press.

Battilana, Julie, and Silvia Dorado. 2010. "Building Sustainable Hybrid Organizations: The Case of Commercial Microfinance Organizations." *Academy of Management Journal* 53 (6): 1419–40.

BBC. 2011. "Cuts 'destroying big society' concept, says CSV head," http://www.bbc.co.uk/news/uk-politics-12378974.

Beem, Christopher. 1999. *The Necessity of Politics: Reclaiming American Public Life*. Chicago: University of Chicago Press.

Bender, Courtney. 2003. *Heaven's Kitchen: God's Love, We Deliver*. Chicago: University of Chicago Press.

Berger, M. 2011. *Répondre en citoyen ordinaire: Enquête sur les engagements profanes dans un dispositif d'urbanisme participatif à Bruxelles*. Doctoral thesis. Brussels: Université Libre de Bruxelles, Department of Sociology.

Berger, Peter, and Thomas Luckman. 1966. *The Social Construction of Reality*. Garden City, NY: Anchor Books.

Blee, Kathleen. 2003. *Inside Organized Racism*. Berkeley and Los Angeles: University of California Press.

Bob, Clifford. 2004. "Marketing Rebellion: Insurgent Groups, International Media, and NGO Support." *International Politics* 38: 311–34.

Bob, Clifford. 2002. "Globalization and the Social Construction of Human Rights Campaigns." In *Globalization and Human Rights*, Alison Brysk, ed., Berkeley and Los Angeles: University of California Press.

Bob, Clifford. 2005. *The Marketing of Rebellion: Insurgents, Media, and International Activism*. New York: Cambridge University Press.

Bok, Derek. 2011. *The Politics of Happiness: What a Government Can Learn From the New Research on Well-Being*. Princeton: Princeton University Press.

Booth, Philip, and Bernard Jouve, eds. 2005. *Metropolitan Democracies*. Burlington, VT: Ashgate.

Bourdieu, Pierre. 1984. *Distinction*. Cambridge, MA: Harvard University Press.

Boyes, Roger. 2009. *Meltdown Iceland*. London: Bloomsbury Publishing.

Breviglieri, Marc. 1999. "L'insupportable. L'excès de proximité, l'atteinte à l'autonomie et le sentiment de violation du privé." In Marc Breviglieri, Claudette Lafaye, and Danny Trom, *Sens de la justice, sens critique*. Paris: Economica.

Bullard, Robert. 2000 [1990]. *Dumping in Dixie: Race, Class, and Environmental Quality*. Boulder, CO: Westview Press.

Butler, Samuel. 1872. *Erewhon*. http://www.gutenberg.org/ebooks/1906.

Carrel, Marion. 2012. *Faire participer les habitants? Les quartiers d'habitat social entre injonction participative et empowerment*. Paris: ENS Editions Lettres et sciences humaines.

Chaves, Mark, Laura Stephens, and Joseph Galaskiewicz. 2004. "Does Government Funding Suppress Nonprofits' Political Activities?" *American Sociological Review* 69: 292–316.

Clemens, Elisabeth. 2010. "In the Shadow of the New Deal: Reconfiguring the Roles of Government and Charity, 1928–1940." In Elisabeth Clemens and Doug Guthrie, eds, *Politics and Partnerships: The Role of Voluntary Associations in America's Political Past and Present*. Chicago: University of Chicago Press.

Cook, Brian. 2011. *Angels of Mercy or Carriers of Conflict? International Humanitarian Organizations and Inter-Group Conflict*. American Sociological Association Annual Meetings, Las Vegas, NV.

Cullather, Nick. 2010. *The Hungry World: America's Cold War Battle Against Poverty in Asia*. Cambridge, MA: Harvard University Press.

References

Dale, John G. 2010. *Free Burma: Transnational Legal Action and Corporate Accountability*. Minneapolis: University of Minnesota Press.

Daniels, Arlene Kaplan. 1988. *Invisible Careers: Women Civic Leaders from the Volunteer World*. Chicago: University of Chicago Press.

Davis, Diane. 2004. *Discipline and Development: Middle Classes and Prosperity in East Asia and Latin America*. New York: Cambridge University Press.

Dekker, Paul and Loek Halman, eds. 2003. *The Values of Volunteering*, 71–90. New York: Kluwer.

Della Porta, Donatella, Massimiliano Andretta, and Lorenzo Mosca. 2006. *Globalization from Below: Transnational Activists and Protest Networks*. Minneapolis, MN: University of Minnesota Press.

Domhoff, G. William. 1975 [2012]. *Bohemian Grove and Other Retreats: A Study in Ruling-Class Cohesiveness*. New York: Harper Collins. (updated 2012 in "Social Cohesion and the Bohemian Grove: The Power Elite at Summer Camp," on Who Rules America online. http://www2.ucsc.edu/who rulesamerica/power/bohemian_grove.html.

Duchin, Ran, and Denis Sosyura. 2012. "The Politics of Government Investment." *Journal of Financial Economics*, 106 (1), October: 24–48.

Duyvendak, Jan Willem, Ellen Grootegoed, and Evelien Tonkens, eds. forthcoming. *Welfare State Reform, Recognition and Emotional Labour.*

Easterlin, Richard. 2010. *Happiness, Growth, and the Life Cycle*. Holger, Hinte and Klaus F. Zimmerman, eds. Bonn, Germany: Institute for the Study of Labor Economics.

Edwards, Michael. 2009. *Civil Society, 2nd edition*. Cambridge: Polity.

Edwards, Michael. 2012. *The Oxford Handbook of Civil Society*. New York: Oxford University Press.

Edwards, Michael, and D. Hulme. 1996. "Introduction: NGO Performance and Accountability." In *Beyond the Magic Bullet: NGO Performance and Accountability in the Post-Cold War World*. London: Kumarian Press.

Eliasoph, Nina. 1998. *Avoiding Politics: How Americans Produce Apathy in Everyday Life*. Cambridge, UK: Cambridge University Press.

Eliasoph, Nina. 2009. "Top-Down Civic Projects Are Not Grassroots Associations: How The Differences Matter in Everyday Life." *Voluntas: International Journal of Voluntary and Nonprofit Organizations*: 20: 291–308.

Eliasoph, Nina. 2011. *Making Volunteers: Civic Life After Welfare's End*. Princeton, NJ: Princeton University Press.

Elyachar, Julia. 2005. *Markets of Dispossession: NGOs, Economic Development and the State in Cairo*. Durham, NC and London: Duke University Press.

Epstein, Barbara. 1993. *Political Protest and Cultural Revolution*. Berkeley and Los Angeles: University of California Press.

Erikson, Erik H. 1959. *Identity and the Life Cycle*. New York: International Universities Press.

169

References

Esping-Anderson, Gøsta. 1990. *The Three Worlds of Welfare Capitalism.* Princeton, NJ: Princeton University Press.

Foucault, Michel. 1989. *The Order of Things.* New York: Routledge.

Freeman, Jo. 1972. "The Tyranny of Structurelessness." *Berkeley Journal of Sociology* 17, 1972–3. http://www.jofreeman.com/joreen/tyranny.htm.

Friedman, Milton, and Rose Friedman. 1980. *Free to Choose.* New York: Harcourt, Brace, Jovanovitch.

Frye, Margaret. 2012. "Bright Futures in Malawi's New Dawn: Educational Aspirations as Assertions of Identity." *American Journal of Sociology* 117 (6): 1565–1624.

Fung, Archon. 2003. "Deliberative Democracy, Chicago-Style: Grassroots Governance in Policing and Education." In Archon Fung and Erik Olin Wright, eds, *Deepening Democracy: Institutional Innovations in Empowered Participation*, 111–43 New York: Verso.

Fung, Archon and Erik Olin Wright, eds. 2003. *Deepening Democracy: Institutional Innovations in Empowered Participation.* New York: Verso.

Galbraith, John Kenneth. 1967. *The New Industrial State.* New York: Houghton-Mifflin.

Gamson, William. 1996. "Safe Spaces and Social Movements." In Gale Miller and James A. Holstein, eds, *Perspectives on Social Problems: A Research Annual*, Vol 8: 27–38. Greenwich, CT: JAI Press.

Garofolo, Pat. 2011. "Since 1950s, Lower Top Tax Rates Have Coincided With Weaker Economic Growth." Think Progress website. June 20, 2011. http://thinkprogress.org/economy/2011/06/20/249061/chart-taxes-economic-growth/?mobile=nc.

Gastil, J. 1993. *Democracy in Small Groups: Participation, Decision-Making and Communication.* Philadelphia, PA: New Society Publishers.

Gaventa, John. 1982. *Power and Powerlessness: Quiescence and Rebellion in an Appalachian Valley.* New York: Oxford University Press.

George, Susan. 1986. *How the Other Half Dies.* New York: Penguin.

Giddens, Anthony. 1991. *Modernity and Self-Identity: Self and Society in the Late Modern Age.* Stanford: Stanford University Press.

Gilman, Charlotte Perkins. 1979 [1915]. *Herland.* New York: Pantheon.

Gitlin, Todd. 1980. *The Whole World is Watching: Mass Media in the Making and Unmaking of the New Left.* Berkeley and Los Angeles: University of California Press.

Glendon, Mary Ann. 1991. *Rights Talk: The Impoverishment of Political Discourse.* New York: Free Press.

Goldman, Emma. 2006. *Vision on Fire: Emma Goldman on the Spanish Revolution.* Oakland, CA: AK Press.

Gorney, Roderic. 1972. *The Human Agenda: How to Be at Home in the Universe – Without Magic.* Los Angeles: The Guild of Tutors Press.

Granovetter, Marc. 1973. "The Strength of Weak Ties." *American Journal of*

References

Sociology, 78 (6), (May): 1360–80.

Gray, Christina. 2012. *Efficient Passions: Care and Justice Ethics in the Context of International Human Rights Organizations*. Doctoral thesis. Los Angeles: University of Southern California, Department of Political Science and International Relations.

Gret, Marion, and Yves Sintomer. 2005. *The Porto Alegre Experiment*. New York: Zed Books.

Gurria, Angel. 2011. "Launch of the OECD Inventory of Estimated Budgetary Support and Tax Expenditures Relating to Fossil Fuels." October 4, 2011, Paris. Opening remarks to Organization of Economic Cooperation and Development's Inventory of Estimated Budgetary Support and Tax Expenditures for Fossil Fuels.

Haase, Dwight. 2012. "Banking on the Poor." *Contexts* 11 (1), Winter: 36–41.

Habermas, Jürgen. 1985. *Theory of Communicative Action*, Vol. 2. Cambridge: Polity.

Hall, Peter Dobkin. 2006. "Nonprofit, Voluntary, and Religious Entities." In Susan B. Carter et al., eds, *Historical Statistics of the United States: Earliest Times to the Present, Millennial Edition, Vol. 2, part B*. New York: Cambridge University Press.

Hamidi, Camille. 2006. "Eléments pour une approche interactionniste de la politisation: engagement associatif et rapport au politique dans des associations locales issues de l'immigration." *Revue Française de Science Politique* 56 (1): 5–25.

Haney, Lynne. 2010. *Offending Women: Power, Punishment, and the Regulation of Desire*. Berkeley and Los Angeles: University of California Press.

Hashemi, Syed, Sidney Ruth Schuler, and Ann Riley. 2004. "Rural Credit Programs and Women's Empowerment in Bangladesh." *World Development* 24 (4): 635–53.

Harvey, David. 1990. *The Condition of Postmodernity*. New York: Blackwell Publishers.

Helander, Voitto, and Susan Sundback. 1998. "Defining the Nonprofit Sector: Finland." Lester M. Salamon and Helmut K. Anheier, eds, *Working Papers of the Johns Hopkins Comparative Nonprofit Sector Project*, no. 34, Baltimore: The Johns Hopkins Institute for Policy Studies.

Hendrickson, Mark. 2010. "Steering the State: Government, Nonprofits, and the Making Labor Knowledge in the New Era." In Elisabeth Clemens and Doug Guthrie, eds, *Politics and Partnerships: The Role of Voluntary Associations in America's Political Past and Present*. Chicago: University of Chicago Press.

Heritage, Timothy. 2012. "Philanthropist Billionaire Transforms Georgian Politics." Reuters, June 7, 2012. http://www.reuters.com/article/2012/06/07/us-georgia-opposition-idUSBRE8560K220120607.

Herman, Edward, and Noam Chomsky. 1989. *Manufacturing Consent*. New York: Pantheon.

References

Hermes, Joke. 2006. "Citizenship in the Age of the Internet." *European Journal of Communication* 21 (3): 295–309.

Hightower, Jim. 2012. "Cooperatives over Corporations." February 24. Retrieved from http://www.truth-out.org/cooperatives-over-corporations/1330091031.

Hillman, Arthur. 1960. *Neighborhood Centers Today: Action Programs for a Rapidly Changing World*. New York: National Federation of Settlements and Neighborhood Centers.

Hobsbawm, Eric. 1962. *The Age of Revolution: 1789–1848*. New York: New American Library.

Huxley, Aldous. 1962. *Island*. New York: Harper Collins. http://www.huxley.net/island/.

Jensen, Jane, and Susan D. Phillips. 2000. "Distinctive Trajectories: Homecare and the Voluntary Sector in Quebec and Ontario." In Keith G. Banting, ed., *The Nonprofit Sector in Canada: Roles and Relationships*. Montreal and Kingston: McGill-Queen's University Press.

Kameo, Nahoko. 2010. *Empowerment in a Knowledge-Based Workplace: Its Intentions and Consequences*. Masters dissertation. Los Angeles: University of California, Los Angeles, Department of Sociology.

Keck, Margaret, and Kathryn Sikkink. 1998. *Activists Beyond Borders*. Ithaca, NY: Cornell University Press.

Ketcham, Christopher. 2011. "The New Populists." *American Prospect*. December 12, 2011. http://prospect.org/article/new-populists-0

Khan, Shamus. 2011. *Privilege: The Making of an Adolescent Elite at St Paul's School*. Princeton, NJ: Princeton University Press.

King, Martin Luther. 1963. "Letter from a Birmingham Jail." Retrieved from Martin Luther King Junior Online, August 2012. http://www.mlkonline.net/jail.html.

Kittay, Eva Feder. 2000. "When Care is Just and Justice is Caring: The Case of the Care for the Mentally Retarded." *Public Culture* 13 (3): 557–79.

Klein, Ezra. 2012. "A rich guy's case for (much) higher taxes." *Washington Post*, April 17, 2012. http://www.washingtonpost.com/blogs/ezra-klein/post/a-rich-guys-case-for-much-higher-taxes/2012/04/17/gIQA384rNT_blog.html.

Kreiss, Daniel. 2012. *Taking Our Country Back: The Crafting of Networked Politics from Howard Dean to Barack Obama*. New York: Oxford University Press.

Kunda, Gideon. 1992. *Engineering Culture: Control and Commitment in a High Tech Corporation*. Philadelphia, PA: Temple University Press.

Lagarde, Christine. 2011. "The Arab Spring, One Year On." *The Huffington Post*, December 6, 2011.

Lakoff, George. 1987. *Women, Fire and Dangerous Things*. Chicago: University of Chicago Press.

Lang, Amy. 2007. "But Is It for Real? The British Columbia Citizens' Assembly as a Model of State-Sponsored Civic Empowerment." *Politics and Society* 35 (1): 35–69.

References

Lappé, Frances Moore, Joseph Collins, and Peter Rosset, with Luis Esparza. 1998. *World Hunger: 12 Myths*, 2nd edn. New York: Grove Press/Earthscan.

Laville, Jean-Louis, Benoit Levesque, and Marguerite Mendell. 2006. *The Social Economy: Diverse approaches and practices in Europe and Canada*. Cahier de l'ARUC-ÉS. Bibliothèque et Archives nationales du Québec.

Lee, Caroline. 2010. "Civic-izing Markets: Selling Social Profits in Public Deliberation." Paper given at Democratizing Inequalities Conference. NYU, Center for Public Knowledge, NY, October 2010.

Lee, Caroline. forthcoming. *Disciplining Democracy: Public Engagement Experts and the New Participatory Economy*.

Leonard, J. T. 2007. "Schlafly Cranks Up Agitation at Bates." *Lewiston-Auburn Sun Journal*, March 29, 2007. http://www.sunjournal.com/node/682725.

Leonhardt, David. 2012. "There's Still Hope for the Planet." *New York Times*, July 21, 2012. http://www.nytimes.com/2012/07/22/sunday-review/a-ray-of-hope-on-climate-change.html.

Lichterman, Paul. 1996. *The Search for Political Community: American Activists Reinventing Community*. Cambridge, UK: Cambridge University Press.

Lim, Alwyn. 2012. *The Globalization of Corporate Social Responsibility – Emergence, Diffusion, and Reception of Global Corporate Governance Frameworks*. Doctoral thesis. Ann Arbor: University of Michigan, Department of Sociology.

Lorentzen, Hakon, and Lesley Hustinx. 2007. "Civic Involvement and Modernization." *Journal of Civil Society* 3 (2): 101–18.

Luhtakallio, Eeva, Marion Carrel, and Nina Eliasoph. 2011. "Researching Bike Activism." Unpublished paper.

Luque, Emilio. 2005. "Researching Environmental Citizenship and its Publics." *Environmental Politics* 14 (2): 211–25.

McAdam, Doug. 1990. *Freedom Summer*. New York: Oxford University Press.

McArthur, Benjamin. 1975. "The Chicago Playground Movement: A Neglected Feature of Social Justice." *Social Service Review* 49 (3): 376–95.

McPherson, J. Miller, and Lynn Smith-Lovin. 1987. "Homophily in Voluntary Organizations: Status Distance and the Composition of Face-to-Face Groups." *American Sociological Review* 52 (3): 370–9.

Makarova, Katja. 1998. "The Mahalla, Civil Society and the Domestication of the State in Uzbekistan". Paper presented at the annual conference of the Association for the Study of Nationalities, New York, April 1998.

Mansbridge, Jane. 1980. *Beyond Adversary Democracy*. Chicago: University of Chicago Press.

Marshall, T. H. 1998 [1958]. "Citizenship and Social Class." In Gershon Shafir, ed., *The Citizenship Debate*. Minneapolis, MN: University of Minnesota Press.

Martens, Kerstin. 2002. "Mission Impossible? Defining Non-Governmental Organisations." *Voluntas: International Journal of Voluntary and Nonprofit Organisations* 13 (3), September 2002: 271–85.

References

Marwell, Nicole P. 2004. "Privatizing the Welfare State: Nonprofit Community-Based Organizations as Political Actors." *American Sociological Review*, 69: 265–91.

Mayer, Jane. 2010. "Covert Operations: The billionaire brothers who are waging a war against Obama." *The New Yorker*, August 30, 2010. Retrieved December 15, 2011. http://www.newyorker.com/reporting/2010/08/30/100830fa_fact_mayer#ixzz1pWCY2eNo.

Mead, Margaret. 1971 [1928]. *Coming of Age in Samoa*. New York: Harper Perennial.

Merton, Robert. 1938. "Social Structure and Anomie." *American Sociological Review* 3: 672–82.

Minkoff, Debra C. 2002. "The Emergence of Hybrid Organizational Forms: Combining Identity-based Service Provision and Political Activism." *Nonprofit and Voluntary Sector Quarterly* 31 (3) (September): 377–401.

Mishkin, Frederic, and Tryggvi Thor Herbertsson. 2006. *Financial Stability in Iceland*. Reykjavik, Iceland: Icelandic Chamber of Commerce.

Morgan, Robin. 1979. *Going Too Far: The Personal Chronicle of a Feminist*. New York: Vintage Books.

Moynihan, Daniel Patrick. 1970. *Maximum Feasible Misunderstanding: Community Action in the War on Poverty*. New York: Free Press.

Musso, Juliet, with Christopher Weare, Nail Oztas, and William E. Loges. 2006. "Neighborhood Governance Reform and Networks of Community Power in Los Angeles." *American Review of Public Administration* 36 (1).

National Taxpayers Union. 2012. "History of Federal Individual Income Bottom and Top Bracket Rates." http://www.ntu.org/tax-basics/history-of-federal-individual-1.html.

Nelson, Barbara. 1986. *Making an Issue of Child Abuse*. Chicago: Chicago University Press.

Noguera, Pedro, ed. 2006. *Beyond Resistance! Youth Activism and Community Change*. New York: Routledge.

Norgaard, Kari. 2011. *Living in Denial: Climate Change, Emotions, and Everyday Life*, Cambridge, MA: MIT Press.

Nussbaum, Martha. 2001. *The Fragility of Goodness: Luck and Ethics in Greek Tragedy and Philosophy*. New York: Cambridge University Press.

O'Connor, Alice. 2010. "Bringing the Market Back In: Philanthropic Activism and Conservative Reform." In Elisabeth Clemens and Doug Guthrie, eds, *Politics and Partnerships: The Role of Voluntary Associations in America's Political Past and Present*. Chicago: University of Chicago Press.

Occupy Wall Street. 2012. *General Assembly Guide*. Retrieved February 3, 2012 from http://peopleslibrary.wordpress.com/2011/10/05/general-assembly-guide/.

Oliver, Eric. 2001. *Democracy in Suburbia*. Princeton, NJ: Princeton University Press.

References

Oreskes, Naomi, and Erik M. Conway. 2010. *Merchants of Doubt: How a Handful of Scientistst Obscured the Truth on Issues from Tobacco Smoke to Global Warming*. New York: Bloomsbury Press.

Orlov, Dmitry. 2008. *Reinventing Collapse: The Soviet Example and American Prospects*. Gabriola Island, BC, Canada: New Society Publishers.

Parreñas, Rhacel. 2011. *Illicit Flirtations: Labor, Migration, and Sex Trafficking in Tokyo*. Stanford: Stanford University Press.

Pennock, Michael, and Dasho Karma Ura. 2007. The Gross National Happiness Abridged Survey. Paper given at Third International Conference on Gross National Happiness, Chulalongkorn University, Bangkok, Thailand.

Perks, Rob. 2009. "Appalachian Heartbreak: Time to End Mountaintop Removal Coalmining." National Resources Defense Council http://www.nrdc.org/land/appalachian/default.asp. Last revised 11/9/2009.

Pettinicchio, David. 2011. "Explaining the Emergence of the Disability Rights Movement." Collective Behavior and Social Movements Workshop, Las Vegas, August.

Pitkin, Hannah. 1980. "Justice: On Relating Private and Public." *Political Theory* 9 (3): 327–352.

Polanyi, Karl. 2001 [1944]. *The Great Transformation: The Political and Economic Origins of Our Time*. Boston: Beacon Press.

Polletta, Francesca. 2002. *Freedom Is an Endless Meeting: Democracy in American Social Movements*. Chicago: University of Chicago Press.

Polletta, Francesca, Pang Ching, Bobby Chen, Beth Gardner, and Alice Motes. forthcoming. "Is the Web Creating New Reasons to Protest?" In Bert Klandermans, Jacquelien Steklenburg, and Conny Roggeband, eds, *Advances in Social Movement Theory*. Minneapolis, MN: University of Minnesota Press.

Poppendieck, Janet. 1999. *Sweeet Charity: Emergency Food and the End of Entitlement*. New York: Penguin.

Potts, C. Brady. 2012. *Enduring Disaster: Social Theodicy in Response to Three Gulf Coast Hurricanes, 1900–2005*. Doctoral thesis. Los Angeles: University of Southern California, Department of Sociology.

Psihopaidas, Demetrios. 2012. *Gender, Sexuality, and the Family: (Re)constructing Morality in Everyday Life*. Masters dissertation. Los Angeles: University of Southern California, Department of Sociology.

Putnam, Robert. 2000. *Bowling Alone*. New York: Simon & Schuster.

Reynolds, Malvinia. 1964. *"It Isn't Nice."* Berkeley, CA: Schroder Music Company.

Rhodes, Jean, and Jean Grossman. 2002. "The Test of Time: Predictors and Effects of Duration in Youth Mentoring Relationships." *American Journal of Community Psychology* 30: 199–206.

Rudolf, John. 2012. "Police Tactics In Occupy Protests Vary From Crackdowns To 'Peaceful Coexistence.'" *Huffington Post*, March 7, 2012.

Ryan, William. 1976. *Blaming the Victim*. New York: Vintage.

References

Salamon, Lester, and Helmut Anheier. 1996. *The Emerging Nonprofit Sector: An Overview*. New York: St Martin's Press.

Salamon, Lester, and Helmut Anheier. 1997. *The Nonprofit Sector in the Developing World*. Manchester: Manchester University Press.

Salamon, Lester M. and Wojciech Sokolowski. 2001. "Volunteering in Cross-National Perspective: Evidence From 24 Countries." *Working Papers of the Johns Hopkins Comparative Nonprofit Sector Project*, no. 40. Baltimore: The Johns Hopkins Center for Civil Society Studies.

Salamon, Lester, and Wojciech Sokolowski. 2004. *Global Civil Society: Dimensions of the Nonprofit Sector*, Volume Two. Bloomfield, CT: Kumarian Press.

Salamon, Lester, and Wojciech Sokolowski. 2005. "Institutional Roots of Volunteering: Toward a Macro-Structural Theory of Individual Voluntary Action." In Paul Dekker and Loek Halman, eds, *The Values of Volunteering*, 71–90. New York: Kluwer.

Sampson, Steven. 1996. "The Social Life of Projects: Importing Civil Society to Albania." In Chris Hann and Elizabeth Dunn, eds, *Civil Society: Challenging Western Models*. New York: Routledge.

Schor, Juliet, 1992. *The Overworked American: The Unexpected Decline in Leisure*. New York: Basic Books.

Schudson, Michael. 1997. "Why Conversation Is Not the Soul of Democracy." *Critical Studies in Mass Communication* 14: 297–309.

Schudson, Michael. 1998. *The Good Citizen: A History of American Civic Life*. New York: Martin Kessler Books.

Schudson, Michael. 2006. "The Trouble with Experts – and Why Democracies Need Them." *Theory and Society* 35: 491–506.

Schuman, Howard, and Stanley Presser. 1997. *Questions and Answers in Attitude Surveys*. Thousand Oaks, CA: Sage.

Scott, James C. 1989. *Domination and the Arts of Resistance*. New Haven, CT: Yale University Press.

Sigurgeirsdóttir, Silla, and Robert H. Wade. 2011. "Iceland's Loud No." *Le Monde Diplomatique*, retrieved March 12, 2012 from http://mondediplo.com/2011/08/02iceland.

Sirianni, Carmen, and Lewis Friedland. 2001. *Civic Innovation in America: Community Empowerment, Public Policy, and the Movement for Civic Renewal*. Berkeley: University of California Press.

Skocpol, Theda. 1995. *Protecting Soldiers and Mothers: The Political Origins of Social Policy in United States*. Cambridge, MA: Harvard University Press.

Skocpol, Theda. 2003. *Diminished Democracy: From Membership to Management in American Civic Life*. Norman: University of Oklahoma Press.

Skocpol, Theda, and Morris Fiorina. 1999. *Civic Engagement in American Democracy*. Washington, DC: Brooking Institute.

Smith, Steven Rathgeb, and Michael Lipsky. 1995. *Nonprofits for Hire: The*

References

Welfare State in the Age of Contracting. Cambridge, MA: Harvard University Press.

Sobieraj, Sara, and Deborah White. 2004. "Taxing Political Life: Reevaluating the Relationship between Voluntary Association Membership, Political Engagement, and the State." *Sociological Quarterly* 45 (4): 739–64.

Spires, Anthony. 2011. "Organizational Homophily in International Grantmaking: US-Based Foundations and their Grantees in China." *Journal of Civil Society* 7 (3): 305–31.

Stauber, John, and Sheldon Rampton. 1996. *Toxic Sludge is Good for You: Lies, Damn Lies, and the Public Relations Industry.* Monroe, Maine: Common Courage Press.

Stiglitz, Joseph, Amartya Sen, and Jean-Paul Fitoussi. 2010. *Mismeasuring Our Lives: Why GDP Doesn't Add Up.* New York: New Press.

Swidler, Ann. 2006. "Syncretism an Subversion in AIDS Governance: How Locals Cope with Global Demands." *International Affairs* 82 (2) (March): 269–84.

Swidler, Ann, and Susan Cott Watkins. 2006. "Ties of Dependence: AIDS and Transactional Sex in Rural Malawi." *Studies in Family Planning* 38 (3) (September): 147–62.

Swidler, Ann and Susan Cott Watkins. 2009. "'Teach a Man to Fish': The Doctrine of Sustainability and its Effects on Three Strata of Malawian Society." *World Development* 37 (7) (July):1182–1196

Talpin, Julien. 2007. *Schools of Democracy: How Ordinary Citizens Become Competent in Participatory Budgeting Institutions.* Doctoral thesis. Florence: European University Institute.

Terriquez, Veronica. forthcoming. "Civic Inequalities?: Race/Ethnicity, Immigrant Incorporation, and Latina Mothers' Participation in their Children's Schools." *Sociological Perspectives.*

Thomas Isaac, T. M., and Patrick Heller. 2003. "Democracy and Development: Decentralized Planning in Kerala." In Archon Fung and Erik Olin Wright, eds, *Deepening Democracy: Institutional Innovations in Empowered Participation.* New York: Verso.

Tocqueville, Alexis de. 1968 [1835]. *Democracy in America,* ed. J. P. Mayer. New York: Anchor Books.

Tocqueville, Alexis de. 1961 [1835]. *De la démocratie en Amérique.* Paris: Editions Gallimard.

Tronto, Joan. 1994. *Moral Boundaries: A Political Argument for an Ethic of Care.* New York: Routledge.

Tyler, Jeff. 2012. "Banks demolish foreclosed homes, raise eyebrows." *American Public Media.* Retrieved October 14, 2012. http://www.marketplace.org/topics/business/banks-demolish-foreclosed-homes-raise-eyebrows.

Verba, Sidney, Kay Schlozman, and Henry Brady. 1996. *Voice and Equality: Civic Voluntarism in American Politics.* Cambridge, MA: Harvard University Press.

References

Wagner, David. 1989. "Radical Movements in the Social Services: A Theoretical Framework." *Social Service Review* 63 (2) (June): 264–84.

Walker, Edward T. 2009. "Privatizing Participation: Civic Change and the Organizational Dynamics of Grassroots Lobbying Firms." *American Sociological Review* 74: 83–105.

Walker, Edward T. 2010. "Legitimating the Corporation Through Participation." Paper given at Democratizing Inequalities Conference. NYU, Center for Public Knowledge, New York, October 2010.

Walker, Edward T. forthcoming. *Grassroots for Hire: How Strategic Public Affairs Consultants are Reshaping Participation and Policy*. New York: Cambridge University Press.

Walzer, Michael. 1980. *Radical Principles: Reflections of an Unreconstructed Democrat*. New York: Basic Books.

Wheeler, Brian. 2005. "The politics of volunteering" BBC World News, 2 June. http://news.bbc.co.uk/2/hi/uk_news/politics/4576541.stm.

Wherry, Frederick. 2012. *The Culture of Markets*. Cambridge: Polity.

Whyte, William Foote, and Kathleen King Whyte. 1991. *Making Mondragon: The Growth and Dynamics of the Worker Cooperative Complex*. Ithaca, NY: Cornell University Press.

Wilkenson, Richard, and Kate Pickett. 2010. *The Spirit Level: Why Greater Equality Makes Societies Stronger*. New York: Bloomsbury Press.

Wuthnow, Robert. 1999. *Loose Connections: Joining Together in America's Fragmented Communities*. Cambridge, MA: Harvard University Press.

Zacharzewski, Anthony. 2010. "Democracy Pays: How Democratic Engagement Can Cut the Cost of Government." Brighton, UK: The Democratic Society and Public-i.

Zavis, Alexandra. 2010. "Homeboy Industries gets $1.3–million county contract." *Los Angeles Times*, September 15. (retrieved Dec. 2009. http://articles. latimes.com/2010/sep/15/local/la-me-homeboy-industries-20100914).

Index

Index

Index

consensus decision-making 145–6
consumerism 19
cooperative movement 33–7
corporate social responsibility (CSR) 55, 149–50
corporations
  and Astroturf campaigns 132–6
  power of 5, 130
  and the powerlessness of ordinary people 160–1
critics of volunteering 1–2
CSR (corporate social responsibility) 55, 149–50

Dahl, Robert 47, 48
democracy 4, 9–42
  defining 6
  the democratic experiment 63
  dystopias and failures of 158–61
  and equality 18–20, 37–40, 129
  and eudaimonea 41
  and human nature 163
  and internet-based activism 148
  participatory 136, 151–7
  political activism and volunteering 57–9
  and practical problem-solving 40
  social citizenship and the welfare state 77–81
  and the state 65, 72, 158
  and the tyranny of the majority 16–18
  and wealth 37
  and working-class politics 138
  see also Tocqueville, Alexis de; workplace democracy
dependence
  Tocqueville on democracy and the fear of 13–16
deregulation
  financial services in the US 85
  formerly state-run enterprises 67–8
  Icelandic banks 86–7
development projects
  dangers of centralized planning 74–7
disability rights movement 2, 48–9

disaster relief organizations 120–1
diversity
  and personal transformation projects 114–15
  and safe spaces 147
donations
  and empowerment projects 112–15, 117–18, 119
  civic self-help 105–6
  marketing cultures to faraway donors 110–11
dystopias 158–61

economy
  and aristocracy of industry 20–1
  civic associations and the state 66–9, 73, 76–7, 92
  competition and equality 19–20
  defining the term 5
  and government 7
  government funding and economic growth 92–3
  measuring GDP 89–90
  and participatory democracy 154
education
  governments and the market 64, 77
  see also schools
egalitarianism 9
Eisenhower, Dwight D. 83
elites
  and civic self-help projects 101–3
  and the "dominant ideology" 138–9
  and inequality in civic participation 130–6
  and local cultures 107–8, 109–10
emotional benefits of civic associations 12, 13
emotionally transformative, volunteering as 28–9
employment protection 30–1
empowerment projects 98–128, 158–9, 162
  cherry-picking 106, 115
  civic self-help 98, 99–107
  and conflict 155–6
  and experts 115–22

181

Index

Index

Index

medieval Europe
  hierarchies of dependence and
    attachment in 13–14
Mexico
  civic associations rates 70
  immigration to the US from 28–9
  indigenous people and civic
    engagement 94–5
micro-finance movement 103–4
Mismeasuring Our Lives (Stiglitz, Sen
  and Fitoussi) 91
mob rule 17
moral luck 41, 49
Morgan Stanley 134
mountaintop removal
  and centralized decision-making
    74–5, 76
multicultural literature 113
multiculturalist societies
  and the private/public divide
    54–5

naming social problems 45–7
national federations
  and egalitarian policy changes
    58–9
Nature
  and decision-making 163–4
neo-liberalism
  and empowerment projects 126–8
Netherlands
  participatory democracy in 155
New Zealand 69
newspaper reports
  on Occupy activists 57
NGOs (non-governmental
    organizations) 2, 3, 94–125,
    162
  advocacy organizations 122
  budgets 94
  defining 96–8
  definition and examples of 5–6
  and food activism 62
  funding 116
  and governments 5–6, 96, 97, 98,
    106
  mismatched missions of 3

NGO-ization of civic engagement
    158
  overturning of corporate and
    government policies by 94–5
  routes to becoming an NGO 98
  social service NGOs 125–6
  and the Tocquevillean ideal of civic
    associations 94, 96–7
  worldwide growth of 95–6
  see also empowerment projects
Nigeria
  oil minorities and Royal Dutch
    Shell 3, 95, 109–10, 126
nobility
  democracy and dependence 14
nonprofit organizations *see*
    NGOs (non-governmental
    organizations)
Nordic countries
  governments and civic associations
    64–5, 92
  and social citizenship 78–9
northern European countries
  states and civic associations 69, 71
northern Italy
  civic associations in 68–9
Norway 3
novels
  novel-reading 60, 62
  portrayal of civic clubs in 58–9
  utopian 53–4, 80
nutrition advice
  civic self-help projects 104–5

Obama online campaign 148
Occupy movement 2, 50, 52, 57,
    85–6, 162
  consensus decision-making 146
  and inequality in civic participation
    130
  and progress 89
  spokespeople 145
  opening up civic participation
    143–57
  consensus and leaderless groups
    144–6
  internet activism 136, 147–9

185

Index

Index